THE DESIGNED SELF
Psychoanalysis and Contemporary Identities

Relational Perspectives Book Series
Volume 27

Relational Perspectives Book Series

Lewis Aron and Adrienne Harris
Series Editors

Volume 1
Rita Wiley McCleary-*Conversing with Uncertainty: Practicing Psychotherapy in a Hospital Setting*

Volume 2
Charles Spezzano-*Affect in Psychoanalysis: A Clinical Synthesis*

Volume 3
Neil Altman-*The Analyst in the Inner City: Race, Class, and Culture Through a Psychoanalytic Lens*

Volume 4
Lewis Aron-*A Meeting of Minds: Mutuality in Psychoanalysis*

Volume 5
Joyce A. Slochower-*Holding and Psychoanalysis: A Relational Perspective*

Volume 6
Barbara Gerson, ed.-*The Therapist as a Person: Life Crises, Life Choices, Life Experiences, and Their Effects on Treatment*

Volume 7
Charles Spezzano & Gerald J. Gargiulo, eds.-*Soul on the Couch: Spirituality, Religion, and in Contemporary Psychoanalysis*

Volume 8
Donnel B. Stern-*Unformulated Experience: From Dissociation to Imagination in Psychoanalysis*

Volume 9
Stephen A. Mitchell-*Influence and Autonomy in Psychoanalysis*

Volume 10
Neil J. Skolnick & David E. Scharff, eds.-*Fairbairn, Then and Now*

Volume 11
Stuart A. Pizer-*Building Bridges: Negotiation of Paradox in Psychoanalysis*

Volume 12
Lewis Aron & Frances Sommer Anderson, eds.-*Relational Perspectives* on the Body

Volume 13
Karen Maroda-*Seduction, Surrender, and Transformation: Emotional Engagement in the Analytic Process*

Volume 14
Stephen A. Mitchell & Lewis Aron, ed.-*RelationalPsychoanalysis: The Emergence of a Tradition*

Volume 15
Rochelle G. K. Kainer-*The Collapse of the Self and Its Therapeutic Restoration*

Volume 16
Kenneth A. Frank-*Psychoanalytic Participation: Action, Interaction, and Integration*

Volume 17
Sue Grand-*The Reproduction of Evil: A Clinical and Cultural Perspective*

Volume 18
Steven Cooper-*Objects of Hope: Exploring Possibility and Limit in Psychoanalysis*

Volume 19
James S. Grotstein-*Who Is the Dreamer Who Dreams the Dream?*

Volume 20
Stephen A. Mitchell-*Relationality: From Attachment to Intersubjectivity*

Volume 21
Peter Carnochan-*Looking for Ground: Countertransference, Epistemology, and the Problem of Value*

Volume 22
Muriel Dimen-*Sexuality, Intimacy, Power*

Volume 23
Susan W. Coates, Jane L. Rosenthal, & Daniel S. Schechter, eds.-*September 11: Trauma and Human Bonds*

Volume 24
Randall Lehmann Sorenson-*Minding Spirituality*

Volume 25
Adrienne Harris-*Gender as Soft Assembly*

Volume 26
Emanuel Berman-*Impossible Training: A Relational Psychoanalytic View of Clinical Training and Supervision*

Volume 27
Carlo Strenger-*The Designed Self: Psychoanalysis and Contemporary Identities*

Volume 28
Lewis Aron and Adrienne Harris, eds.-*Relational Psychoanalysis, Vol. II*

THE DESIGNED SELF
Psychoanalysis and Contemporary Identities

CARLO STRENGER

THE ANALYTIC PRESS

2005 Hillsdale, NJ London

Published by The Analytic Press, Inc.
101 West Street, Hillsdale, NJ 07642
www.analyticpress.com

Library of Congress Cataloging-in-Publication Data

Strenger, Carlo.
The designed self : psychoanalysis and contemporary identities / Carlo Strenger.
p. cm. — (Relational perspectives book series ; v. 27)
Includes bibliographical references and index.
ISBN 0-88163-419-0
1. Identity (Psychology) 2. Psychoanalysis 3. Identity (Psychology)—Case studies 4. Psychoanalysis—Case studies. I. Title. II. Series

BF697.S855 2005
155.2'5—dc22

2004054430

Printed in the United States of America
10 9 8 7 6 5 4 3 2 1

In memory of my father,
Dr. Enrico Strenger (1931–2001)

Acknowledgments

This book has been in the making for some four years. Many people have contributed to it directly and indirectly, and I can thank only some of them.

– For many years I have had endless discussions about pretty much everything on earth with Elazar Sturm. The search for meaning in a culture without depth has been one of our recurring topics. This dialogue and our friendship have been invaluable both for this book and for my life.
– Most of this book was written while Helit Ben-Israel and I shared our lives. Not only did she listen patiently to my often interminable ruminations, but, being a gifted member of Generation X herself, she often elucidated issues for me from a perspective shaped by personal experience, intelligence and feeling. Many thanks for everything, including our friendship today.
– Jacob Burak has provided me with important insights into the entrepreneurial culture that has evolved in the 1990s. For this, and for our partnership in researching the psychology of entrepreneurship, many thanks.
– Rafi Gidron has been a great friend, also in difficult times, and I have learned a lot from him about the complexities of high-tech entrepreneurship that has become so iconic of global culture and economy.
– Yariv Horowitz I have spent many hours participating in, laughing at, and musing about Tel Aviv's intense night-life, and the way it combines the allure of endless promise and existential despair. He also taught me a lot about his work as a film director, the world of media, and the movie industry and has deepened my understanding of another facet of the world we live in.
– Maya Negri has been a wonderful presence in my life and has given me the privilege to see the blossoming of a wonderful talent combining creative design and the courage to do her own thing.
– Noah Eyal has been a great friend for years and a valuable partner in dialogue on the quest for identity in Generation X. She also had me meet some of her friends, whose input was helpful.
– My students at Tel Aviv University, who were born into the culture that is the subject of this book, have provided me with lively reactions

and commentary on my thoughts, and made my life richer and more enjoyable.

– My special thanks go to "Iris," "Ben," "Yaron," "Amos," "Ruth," and "Anne," the patients whose stories form the backbone of this book. Working with them therapeutically was deeply gratifying. They have all read, commented on, and approved the publication of their respective stories, and were part of the process of reinventing biographies that preserve the essence of their stories while protecting their identities.
– The owners and staff of "Cafe Noir and of Café Alkalay" have provided me with surroundings and hospitality for many hours of writing. They are part of the Tel Aviv cultural scene and nightlife, which has afforded me many of the insights into the historical present developed in this book. In many ways this book is a tribute to Tel Aviv, its vibrancy, and its contribution to my life for 15 years.

I would also like to thank:

– Lewis Aron, editor of the *Relational Perspectives Book Series,* for his support and generosity of mind.
– Paul E. Spepansky, Managing Director of The Analytic Press, for his enthusiasm in accepting this book for publication.
– Eleanor Starke Kobrin (Lenni), TAP's Managing Editor, for her wonderful dedication in editing this book.
– Joseph Reppen, editor of *Psychoanalytic Psychology* for encouraging me to pursue my own brand of connecting psychoanalytic experience with cultural analysis and for the enjoyable conversations and the friendship.
– Stuart Twemlow, editor of *The International Journal of Applied Psychoanalytic Studies,* for the dialogue and warmth of his support for my ideas over the last several years.
– I am grateful to the publishers of *Psychoanalytic Psychology, International Journal of Applied Psychoanalytic Studies, American Journal of Psychotherapy,* and *Humanistic Psychology* for the permission to reprint material from their journals.
– I presented preliminary versions of the ideas in this book at various conferences, universities, and psychoanalytic institutes. I particularly appreciate the wonderful hospitality and feedback at the Institute of Contemporary Psychoanalysis in Los Angeles in 2001, the important input I received at the 2001 annual conference of the German Psychoanalytic Association, and at the Psychoanalytic Institute in Chicago in 2002.

Contents

Prologue

The Designed Self in the Global Village

This book describes the impact of the far-reaching cultural changes of the last two decades on the process of identity formation. It does so from a vantage point that may seem slightly unlikely: the psychoanalytic consulting room, where people deal with their deepest hopes, fears, terrors, desires, and images of who they would like to be.

My clinical experience of the last decade has led to the hypothesis that the cohort often called Generation X (roughly corresponding to birthdates between 1960 and 1980) lives in a world distinctly different from that of earlier generations, including that of the Baby Boomers, who led the cultural revolution of the 60s and 70s.

Baby Boomers defined their identities through rebellion. They sought freedom in the sexual, intellectual, and cultural domains by conducting an emotionally charged fight against the entrenched values of Western culture. They questioned sexual mores, cultural canons, established authorities, and political realities. Their icons were political revolutionaries like Che Guevara, who fought capitalism; singers like Joan Baez and Bob Dylan, who sang the praises of the new brotherhood of humankind; and artists like Andy Warhol, who rejected the rules of the artistic canon of the West. Their values were formulated by intellectuals like Michel Foucault and Jacques Derrida, who deconstructed the categories that had guided Western culture from politics to the arts.

For the Baby-Boom generation, sexual liberation and the use of drugs were acts of emancipation and a search for new freedom. While severely critical of parental, political, and academic authorities, this generation was engaged in an emotionally highly charged fight against previous generations and their ideals. Having come of age in the unprecedented prosperity of the post-World War II decades, they rejected the values of discipline, austerity, and adaptation to society that had guided their parents. Nevertheless the Baby-Boom revolution was emotionally intensely engaged with the generations, culture, and values that they were fighting.

The children of the Baby-Boom generation, Generation X, were born into a new cultural reality. They no longer had to fight for liberties in the sexual and cultural domain. Their parents no longer took on the role of authorities that had to be and could be fought. The very concept of authority had lost its moorings.

Drugs have ceased to be a way to express rebellion. The use of anything from grass through acid trips to Ecstasy has become no more than a way to spend an enjoyable weekend. Sexual experimentation is no longer a way to define one's identity vis-à-vis one's parents, and it has lost the political subtext embodied in Woodstock's "make love, not war" slogan.

If the parents of Baby Boomers were still trying to impose authority on their children, Baby Boomers, as parents, are bewildered and lost. They fought for freedom and are wary of imposing themselves. As a result, GenXers, are not really engaged in a fight with their parents to define their identities. The ambivalent mix of love and hate, respect and disdain that characterized earlier generations in their rebellion against parents has given way to a faint sense of irrelevance.

GenXers are more likely to turn to the Internet to find out about what's in and what's out than to their own parents. Their cultural frame of reference has lost the vertical orientation that has characterized the transmission of culture through generations. They live in a cultural space created by their contemporaries.

If their parents represent neither present role models nor authorities that need to be rebelled against, what guides GenXers in acquiring personal identities? The answer, I suggest, is that the dominant imperative guiding their lives is "design thy self." Identity is not to be inherited through the continuity of ties to the family, culture, or religion. Global icons like blond British soccer star David Beckham can be an idol for Asians,

Blacks, or Indians no less than for British middle-class boys. TV, magazines, and the Web are more likely to provide GenXers with role models than are revered cultural traditions.

The psychoanalytic consulting room was one of the cultural epicenters of the Western middle classes of the 20th century. Freud's theory of the Oedipus complex condensed the emotional reality of generations that grew up in the hotbed of posttraditional nuclear families. His patients suffered from repressions that were demanded by the restrictive bourgeois European culture of the European fin de siècle. Freud's iconoclastic role consisted in dismantling taboos that governed both discourse and the social practices of his times.

Freud's patients were suffocated by the sacred and by taboos: "A good child doesn't hate her parents." "A decent girl doesn't have wayward sexual desires." "A real man doesn't feel too much affection toward other men." The great themes were passion and guilt. Patients needed to come to terms with their ambivalence toward those they were supposed to love and respect unequivocally. Women, in particular, had to live with the fact that they had highly ambivalent feelings toward those who condemned them to restricted social roles with very little opportunity for self-expression.

The bourgeoisie was filled with the anxiety of being overwhelmed by desires for pleasure that would undermine the capacity for hard work that constituted the foundation for a place in the upper middle classes. Freud's concern was with the price to be paid for the *Kulturleistung* that made civilized existence (à la fin de siècle) possible.

Psychoanalysis offered those whose souls contained too many unnegotiated conflicts a safe, nonjudgmental environment in which they could import civilization into hitherto uncultivated areas of the psyche. *Wo Es war, soll Ich werden* ("Where id was, there ego shall be"). Psychoanalysis was the art of conscious renunciation, the colonization of the deepest layers of the psyche by civilization.

Many contemporary patients suffer not from an overabundance of sacred cows, but from the trivialization of an overwhelming array of possible experiences that have lost their distinctiveness. Videos with the most bizarre forms of sex are as readily available as Zen meditation classes; kabalistic instruction can be had around the corner as easily as classes in French country-style cooking and Tai Chi.

I do not mean to add to the lamentations of neoconservatives who mourn the loss of old-time religion and family values. I am simply trying to address an objective, social fact that Kenneth Gergen (1991) has aptly called the saturated self. Since most potential clients in the big cities do not live in traditional societies, they must consciously choose their life styles. This is one aspect of what the sociologist Anthony Giddens (1991) has argued is to be a central characteristic of late modernity: reflexivity. There is no decision that can be made on traditional grounds alone. Late-modern persons are expected to make their decisions on the basis of conscious deliberation. The result has aptly been called the minimal self: a self without history, without tradition, without commitments that are a matter of course.

Historian of religion Mircea Eliade (1947), in his classic study *The Sacred and the Profane,* argued that the essence of the sacred is order: there is a hierarchy of places, objects, values. There is a hierarchical chain of being. It is this order that has been deconstructed in the three decades since 1968: liberation has succeeded, and the sacred cows are dead. As a result, urban GenXers are less likely to suffer from neurotic symptoms that express unresolved neurotic conflicts. They are, rather, prone to diffuse feelings of confusion, depression, and disorientation. While they do not have to fight established authorities, they need to live up to the demand to create a life that combines financial, professional, and social success, together with having loads of fun and a sexy persona.

If Freud's patients suffered from an overly restrictive upbringing, GenXers are likely to feel the emptiness generated by too many possibilities. Particularly those gifted enough to have many options live with the constant anxiety that they might fail to live sufficiently spectacular lives. In fact, the prevalence of depression and anxiety disorders has been explained by the psyche's inundation with icons of success (Buss 1993). It is much more difficult to maintain a sense of self-esteem when one is confronted daily with images of seemingly achievable sensational success ranging from Bill Gates's billions through soccer star David Beckham's world-wide popularity to Britney Spears's overwhelming success in her late teens.

Reflections on Fatherlessness

In 1967 the dean of post-World War II German psychoanalysis, Alexander Mitscherlich, published a book titled *Towards a Fatherless Society*. It could be said that, in an uncanny way, his title was prescient and that we are currently living in a fatherless society. This is sociologically often true in the sense that many children grow up without the physical presence of a father, either because of divorce or because they were conceived to be raised by a single mother to begin with.

Fatherlessness is a recurring theme in this book. Its preponderance reaches deeper than the particular constellations to be found in this or that family. The paternal role, as Lacan argued, is also a metaphor for a wide-ranging cultural function: besides having the biological and personal component, it is the symbol for cultural authority itself. Lacan (1977) argued that the sum total of linguistic and cultural associations embodied in a subject's language constitutes that person's unconscious. For people born into Western culture, this implies a huge tradition ranging from Judeo-Christian sources, through the tradition that reaches from Greek philosophy through Roman culture and law, through the canon of Western literature, art, philosophy, and science.

This nexus is not just a collection of cultural associations; it also constitutes cultural authority. Western culture is based on canonical works that define what true culture is. The very notion of the canon is of religious origin. It defines the body of texts that are sanctified and thus authoritative; they contain truths that can be interpreted but not disputed. One of the central characteristics of contemporary global culture is that it is devoid of any such canonic notions. No work of art, writing, philosophy, or other cultural production has the status of being one of the definitive works of culture.

I am aware of the problematic aspects of Lacan's male-oriented equation of the paternal metaphor with the transmission of culture and civilization. I use the metaphor (to the extent that is possible) without assuming a nexus to the male gender. The paternal role in this sense is not connected to the transmitter's being male or female, even though, historically, the transmission of culture has been associated with biological fatherhood.

Fatherhood, as it represents a cultural heritage, becomes problematic once the very validity of such a heritage is called into question. If, indeed, as has been argued repeatedly, this notion of heritage and canon has ceased to be culturally valid, the paternal role per se is called into question. It is possibly no coincidence, then, that so much of contemporary cultural lore about how human beings develop focuses on mothers; here, at least, it seems that we are talking about a role that has been unquestioned and untouched by recent cultural developments.

The drama of the conflict between loyalty to one's parents and their tradition and the yearning for freedom is often assumed to be universal. Yet, when we look at the contemporary global village, this issue seems to have evaporated. Parricide seems no longer to be an issue, as the paternal function and the weight of great cultural traditions seem to have vanished. Contemporary global culture provides a stark contrast to the intergenerational dramas of even the recent historical past.

Anne, 24 years old, was referred to me by a friend of hers who had been in treatment with me some years before. During the first few sessions, she, somewhat haltingly, told me about her problems, which centered primarily on relationships with men. She was very good looking, and men would chat her up all the time. She would generally sleep with them soon after meeting them, but, more often than not, they disappeared. Sometimes, when a relationship began to form, the men would tell her after some months that they simply didn't feel her presence and would leave her. She was left with the dreadful feeling that no man who truly got to know her would ever stay.

I came to know only the bare outline of her history. Her father was American, her mother Israeli. They were married when they were rather young and moved to the United States. After about five years of marriage, the mother found out that the father was having an affair with a business colleague. She decided to take her two daughters and move back to Israel, where she had more of a support network. Two years later, when Anne was five years old, the divorce was finalized. Ever since, Anne saw her father, who had meanwhile married his business colleague, twice a year in the United States.

After the first four sessions, Anne began to find it increasingly difficult to talk. She asked me if I could guide her, ask her questions. I tried to understand what her difficulty was. Did she feel that I was critical of her? Did she feel intimidated? Did she feel that I was not interested in what she was saying? Anne simply could not tell me. In her paralysis, all she could feel was a gaping void. Nothing would emerge. I tried everything from expressing empathy for her plight through suggesting hypotheses about what was blocking her. Nothing helped. For a growing portion of the sessions, Anne could not talk much of the time.

I did have a vague idea about what was happening. Anne had told me that for most of her life the highlight of her year was to visit her father in the United States. Her father was an impressive man, physically and mentally imposing. He had built a successful career in the financial world and lived in an impressive apartment on Park Avenue in New York City. His new wife was beautiful and stylish, was emotionally remote, and cared primarily about their elaborate social life.

Anne would arrive in the United States, and her father would pick her up at the airport. They would enter the chauffeured limousine, and, once they sat down, her father would ask her the question that she dreaded: "So, what are you doing with your life?" Anne would inevitably either fall silent or begin to cry. She felt that she had nothing of interest to say to this man who lived with chauffeured limousines, who was sought after in the highest social and business circles, and led (or so it seemed to her) a fascinating life. What could she tell him? That she went to school? That she had friends? What she was considering studying in college? Nothing, absolutely nothing seemed to be a sufficiently important answer to her father.

I suspected that Anne's silence with me was a reenactment of her paralysis when she met with her father. But I simply could not find a way to explore this (or any other) idea with her. I was feeling more and more wary of the sessions with her and even came to dread them. I was out of my depth. I felt guilty: I knew that Anne, who tried to support herself, did not find it easy to pay for the therapy. I felt an urgent need to help her. Yet not only did I not help her, but we did not even manage to talk.

In fact, the situation became progressively worse. After about half a year, most sessions had the same structure. I would show her in and say hello; Anne would sit down; and then a thick, opaque, heavy silence would ensue. I had run out of ways to talk to her, things to say or do. We would sit in our respective armchairs for 45 minutes. I would ask her if there was something she wanted to tell me before we ended, and then we said good bye.

Sometimes Anne would, haltingly, relate another episode in which she had been dumped by another man. But we could do no useful work on it; any attempt at exploration made her fall silent. The only thing that kept me going was that Anne kept coming to the sessions. Week after week, month after month, she would come to these sessions, which, I suspected, were much more difficult for her than they were for me—and they were very difficult for me to bear. I felt that, if Anne could make the effort to come to the therapy, I could not give up on her. And so both of us kept waiting for nine months, during which time hardly a word was spoken. When I left for a vacation or a lecture trip, she would wish me a good trip, and I expressed my hope that she would feel fine. For the rest of the time, nothing would happen.

Then Anne wearily told me about a man who was courting her. He was good looking and warm hearted and seemed to take a genuine interest in her. And, strangely enough (for her), he was still there after two months. She fell silent and then said, "I'm almost disgusted with him." "Why is that?" I asked, surprised. There was, again, some silence. Anne looked at me intently (which she rarely did) and said, "He actually seems to love me. Anyone who loves me must be a complete idiot." I let this sentence sink in and asked Anne, "Are you aware of what you have just said? Do you actually mean that?" Anne again looked at me intently and said, "Yes, of course."

That session was to be the turning point of this therapy. After a few more weeks, Anne could finally tell me that the reason she could not talk during the sessions was that she felt she had nothing of interest to say, that nothing she could talk about was profound and deep, and that she was afraid of disappointing me, of feeling my disdain for her wasting my time.

Now we could finally talk about the way she experienced me and, in many ways, most men she valued. The similarity of this experience to how she felt toward her father came to the fore.

She could speak of how, for a lifetime, she had yearned for recognition by her father but dreaded not receiving it—and, indeed, had failed to do so up to this point. The therapy, after nine months of waiting, was finally born.

Anne was afraid of boring me or of bothering me with insignificant stories about how paralyzed she felt with some new lover of hers. It may be worth pondering the following questions: Why was she less afraid of sitting in my consulting room and saying absolutely nothing? Why was the terror of these hours and hours of silence more bearable for her than simply trying to talk to me? Why did she have to put both of us through this ordeal of silence before she could finally start talking?

From the therapeutic dialogue that was to ensue during the following years, we arrived at some understanding of what had happened. Anne was profoundly convinced that no man she could value would appreciate her. This, for her, was a nonnegotiable given. Nothing I could do or say could change that. Her mother, her sister, and she had retreated into being women who would be abandoned by men. Her mother, in fact, had never even tried to regain her husband's love. Accepting the verdict that he loved another woman, she had packed and left. And Anne's father had done nothing to stop his wife and his daughters from leaving. He seemed simply not to care.

Anne needed to put us through the ordeal of the long wait to find out if, unlike her father, I cared enough to suffer through the months of helplessness and confusion that I experienced. Nothing that I could say would convince her of the seriousness of my commitment. So she tested me by finding out if I would stay, patiently, even though I had no idea about what I was supposed to do.

Anne's father was, in many ways, the dominant figure in her life. He had established this dominance by being absent. There was probably nothing in the world that she wanted more than to be recognized by him as a human being in her own right. She wanted to be seen by him. Throughout her life she had felt that he saw through her, that she existed for him as an abstraction. She was, on paper, his daughter, but she had no distinct identity for him.

Anne was, psychologically speaking, a semiorphan. In a profound sense her father had ceased to exist in her life when she was three years old. Yet, as often happens when a parent disappears early, he assumed mythical proportions. For Anne he became a larger-than-life figure, the man who was the source of all value. Being recognized by him as a valuable human being (he always said that she was his beautiful girl–but that made her feel like a doll) became the mythical source of all value.

It was to take several years until Anne began to see him in a more realistic light, as a man incapable of making emotional contact. She began to see how much he suffered in his present marriage with a woman who was cold some of the time and hysterically angry at others. And, not surprisingly, she began to have real conversations with him.

▒ ▒ ▒ ▒ ▒

Through Anne we have encountered one of the most obvious forms of fatherlessness. Divorce often leads to loss of a father (even though it need not do so)), and, given the dramatic rise in frequency of divorce since the 1960s, broken family ties are a theme that often plays a role in the life histories of those who came of age in the 1980s and 1990s.

We will get to know other forms of fatherlessness throughout this book. Fathers can be absent because they do not know how to relate to their children. Others feel that they have nothing to give. Still others are so preoccupied by their sense of personal failure that they cannot nurture and guide anyone else. And there are fathers who feel that they simply do not understand their children's world, and they are afraid of being authoritarian–so they retreat.

Children and adolescents are flooded with cultural icons and products created by people who often are in their 20s themselves. As a result, GenXers grew up in a cultural universe defined by their contemporaries. As I said before, they often do not even conceive of earlier cultural traditions as something worth relating to. In addition, as we see in chapter 2, the images of the life worth living generated in the mass media and in advertising are largely geared to adolescents and postadolescents. The fashion models that define the iconography of beauty and the stars that dominate Hollywood's universe mostly have an aura of youth. As a result, the process of maturation does not carry many positive connotations but is defined primarily by loss, particularly the loss of sexual attractiveness. The impact on the subjective experience of the life cycle is momentous (Edlis 2003), and the intergenerational nexus that has been at the center of much psychoanalytic theorizing has been weakened considerably.

OVERVIEW OF CHAPTERS AND TOPICS

In the chapters that constitute this book, I tell the story of my encounters with five extraordinarily talented people who, at the time, were between their early 20s and mid-30s. Each has a unique biography; each carries the unconscious memory of interactions with his or her parents; each was born with a potential that struggled to realize itself. But all of them were also shaped by the cultural forces that surrounded their adolescence and early adulthood. I try to capture their individuality in my descriptions, but I also place each of them within the cultural context of the last two decades.

THE SELF AS PERPETUAL EXPERIMENT

Generation Xers are guided by a new imperative, one partially inherited from Baby Boomers: experiment with yourself. Growing into an identity that is preestablished by one's ties with family, nation, and ethnic group is no longer considered valid. It is no coincidence that the group of sports that GenXers have developed runs under the heading of extreme games. These sports have little in common with classical athletic disciplines. They are derived from urban pastimes like rollerblading, skateboarding, and riding BMX bicycles. Their movements are elaborations of ways of playing in the contemporary urban landscapes, or, more precisely, they push those modes of play to the extreme.

Living a life and shaping the self is supposed to be a form of extreme games. Anything from one's professional career, to one's hair color, to one's body shape, to one's sexuality is subject to experimentation. Lives and selves are there to be designed, and contemporary urban culture presents a wide array of styles that can be used. The 60s ideal of "let it all hang out" authenticity has been replaced by the ideal of designing the self.

The darker side of this new space of freedom is located in the high demands it puts on life. If the categorical imperative is to make one's life as interesting and experimental as possible, nothing but high excitement will do. It seems as if only the combination of adventurousness, embodied in anything from snowboarding to bungee jumping, linked to experimentation with nonstandard sex and plenty of drugs, makes a life truly fulfilling. Too many GenXers feel that they have missed the opportunity for a worthwhile life and that they have settled for nerdhood and mediocrity.

Iris, the protagonist of chapter 1, was a young woman who sought my help because she was caught up in a pattern of relationships with men who patronized her. After a first installment of therapy resolved much of this pattern, she returned some years later for further help. She had transformed from an earnest young woman to a flamboyant participant in bustling Tel Aviv nightlife. I place her search for a sense of authorship over her life against the background of a salient feature of contemporary urban culture: the desire to experiment endlessly with the self.

NOBROW CULTURE

John Seabrook (2000) has argued that an essentially new culture–Nobrow culture– has emerged, which has effectively erased the distinction between serious high culture and popular culture. Whereas Baby Boomers rebelled against the idea of a superior Western canon, GenXers do not even see the Western canon as something that is worth fighting against. They seem to live in a universe that has lost any sense of cultural continuity: they live in a nonrelationship to the past, with very little sense that there is a cultural tradition that is either worth fighting or preserving. Fareed Zakaria (2003) has defined this tendency through his formula of the democratization of culture. As opposed to the canonic conception, Nobrow culture does not ask who appreciates a work of art, but how many appreciate it. Hence the subtitle of Seabrook's book: *The Culture of Marketing and the Marketing of Culture.*

If patients born before, say, 1960, seem to have much more stable internalized images of authority, GenXers seem, if anything, to suffer from a lack of any clearly felt authority. Whereas Baby Boomers are often preoccupied with conflicts around rebelling against internal and external authorities, GenXers often yearn for figures that could truly be experienced as authorities.

Alexander Mitscherlich's (1967) prediction that the West is becoming a fatherless society has become eerily real. This is true not only with respect to cultural continuity, but also, in a very concrete way, Western Europe. Single life is becoming an accepted life choice, and, as a result, all its countries have shrinking populations. If there is nothing worth preserving, there seems to be very little value in producing offspring to whom something can be passed on.

Ben, the patient presented in chapter 2, was a rising star in the world of high-tech startups. He felt that he was fooling everyone; he could not quite understand why people accepted him as an authority. The son of a respected academic, he felt that his own authority was devoid of foundations. The gradual consolidation of his self-image is told against the backdrop of one of the fascinating cultural developments of the last two decades: the emergence of Nobrow culture, which rejects the validity of a cultural canon that defines "genuine" as opposed to popular culture. Nobrow culture also raises the question of what happens to young people whose parents, even though dedicated, feel completely out of their depth in trying to understand their children's cultural universe and mental makeup.

The problem of fatherlessness is also one of the topics of chapter 4, where we meet Amos, a brilliantly gifted young man suffering from feelings of emptiness and the fear of being unmasked as a fake and who was on the way to ejecting himself out of a promising academic career. His therapeutic trajectory was aimed at the gradual uncovering of his father's inability to be a father. It also raises complex questions as to the nature of the psychotherapeutic relationship: to what extent is the task of helping patients to find their own voice influenced by the therapist's personality, his deepest beliefs, values, and emotional and intellectual makeup?

The New Body and Sexuality

Generation X came of age during the Reagan–Thatcher era. The sexual revolution was an established social order for GenXers; they did not have to fight for it. Of course, experimentation with sexuality and gender is not new. The Baby Boomers of the 60s and 70s had made this a central aspect of their self-definition. Yet for the 60s generation, sexual experimentation was in many ways an activity with subversive and even revolutionary contexts.

That is no longer the case. Many GenXers have a very relaxed attitude about sexuality, and they see gender roles as much more fluid than did people of earlier times. I see the same difference in the classroom. My students at Tel Aviv University in recent years have been much more capable of discussing issues of gender and sexuality—including various forms of neosexuality—than were students I taught, say, at the end of the 80s. My current students experience the body as the foundation for self-expression, ranging from body building, through tattoos and body piercing, to constant playing with hair style and color. Not even genetic determinants seem to limit who you can be.

The darker side of this seeming paradise of sexual relaxedness comes to the fore when we look at GenXers' attitudes toward their bodies and the issue of aging. Sexual possibilities seem almost unlimited, but the dominant paradigm of sexual attractiveness determined by the media and by advertising has become distinctly postadolescent. Aging has become even more of a terror than it naturally tends to be. Particularly for women, the semianorectic ideal of the faultlessly youthful body has become a source of perpetual pressure. The imperative "shape your body" is becoming a cultural necessity in a culture that makes many who do not correspond to the prevailing ideal feel sexually irrelevant. We see the impact of these anxieties in chapter 1.

The Sky Was the Limit

The New Economy of the 1990s created opportunities unheard of before. Young people created startup companies that were sold a few years later for sums ranging from millions to billions of dollars. The global village seemed to become the ultimate dream for those gifted and motivated enough to use the new opportunities.

The downside of this paradise of unlimited possibilities has been strongly felt by many. The well-publicized success stories of the 1990s make many gifted young people who only have successful, but not outrageously grand, careers feel a little bit like failures. In particular those engaged in the traditional professions feel stupid: they are working hard to earn their degrees and qualifications at an age when others already have made millions. We see the impact of this constellation on Ben (ch 2) and Yaron (ch 3).

Bobo Ideology: The Fusion of Bourgeoisie and Bohemia

In general, the global village seemed to have become a paradise of freedom. A new category, aptly named by David Brooks (2000) Bobos (derived from "Bourgeois Bohemians"), emerged. It seemed no longer necessary to choose between making money and realizing one's innermost self. The fusion between the hippie and the yuppie seemed to become a reality. Hi-tech startups seemed to provide the playing ground for unbounded creativity and self-expression while promising high salaries and stock options that might soon be worth millions.

While Boboism seems to promise the best of possible worlds, it, at the same time, creates a conundrum for the silent majority, who feel that this myth does not work for them. Are Bobos really realizing their innermost selves by working 16-hour days? Has the combination of hippie freedom and yuppie career indeed succeeded in squaring the circle, or is it a cultural myth that has made it easier for companies to demand working hours that make the life of the hard-working investment banker of the 80s into the epitome of leisure?

Yaron (ch 3) came to see me because he was faced with an unbearable quandary. Having joined a company that epitomized the bustling New Economy of the 1990s, he felt that he could not find his place there. He was torn between the feeling that to become a success he had to join the club of startup entrepreneurs and the distinct sense that he was losing his individuality there. In addition to deciphering his complex personal history, I try to show that part of his dilemma represents that of the wider cultural phenomenon of the Bobo.

The Global Village and Ethnicity

The 60s revolution also generated the politics of identity. Groups that had felt oppressed by white, male, Western values began to assert their demand to be recognized as intrinsically valuable. These included racially defined groups like African Americans, genders (women), people with different sexual orientations (gays and lesbians), and a great variety of ethnic groups ranging from Hispanic Americans through Sephardic Jews in Israel to Muslim Croats in the former Yugoslavia.

Yet the politics of identity lives with an uneasy, dialectical relationship toward the global village. The desire for recognition as a distinct group is counterbalanced by the wish to be part of the hype of global culture with its distinct criteria for success: money, status, and recognition of achievement. As we will see, the fusion of ethnic identity and the wish to find a place in a society largely defined by Western standards can create difficult dilemmas.

The difficult, tempestuous, but ultimately beneficial therapeutic journey I shared with Ruth, a woman of Sephardic origin, is recounted in chapter 5. We see there how her wounded self, her depressions, and the dreams of decay that haunted her are as much the result of her personal history as they reflect the tragic history of the relationships between the Ashkenazi elite who founded and governed the state of Israel for most of its existence and the Sephardic immigrants who were relegated to second-rate status for many decades. Even though the context is specifically Israeli, Ruth's story exemplifies a more general point: the complexity of fusing non-Western ethnic origins into an identity defined by the primarily Western culture of the global village.

Psychoanalysis and Contemporary Urban Culture

Psychoanalysis has been prone to isolate the consulting room from its cultural surroundings. Lately there have been fewer attempts to deal with the general cultural environment as Erik Erikson and Alexander Mitscherlich used to do. Julia Kristeva (1993) is one of the notable exceptions, even though I disagree with many of her conclusions.

Psychoanalysis, like many other disciplines in the humanities and social sciences, finds it difficult to deal with the new cultural realities. The easiest way is to resort to the historically ubiquitous pattern of condemning the present generation as shallow and unaware of the treasures of tradition and to denounce it as devoid of depth (e.g., Bloom 1987; Kimball 2000). Not surprisingly, this is a strategy that has been used by some psychoanalytic authors vis-à-vis Generation X (Chasseguet-Smirgel 1984; Kristeva 1993).

I believe that this strategy was never fruitful in the past. Like all previous generations that have been indicted in a wholesale manner, GenXers have already issued rebuttals to these charges (e.g., Holtz 1995; Thau and Hefflin 1997). Wholesale rejection is neither of any use intellectually nor ethically responsible. Without falling into epistemic, moral, and aesthetic relativism, it is certainly more useful to try to understand a new generation's experience and putting it into context.

Unlike Erikson and Mitscherlich, I have neither an integrative theory of the contemporary, global urban psyche nor a unified vision of how the vast cultural changes should influence psychoanalysis. Nevertheless, in the chapter 6, I present some ideas about a potential psychoanalytic culture that accepts the challenge of dealing with the historical present.

Chapter 1

The Self as Perpetual Experiment

CHANGES IN THE GOAL OF ANALYTIC TREATMENT

Western urban culture seems to have turned the self into a locus of experimentation. Commentators like the German philosopher Peter Sloterdijk (1996) and German sociologist Peter Gross (1999) have argued that Nietzsche's imperative to create one's self rather than just finding it, is rapidly becoming a dominant ethos. From body piercing through S&M, from mind-expanding drugs to creating new forms of religious ritual and experience, the global village seems to be turning into a space for endless experimentation. Foucault's (1984) post-Nietzschean dictum that the self should be treated like a work of art in progress seems to have become the norm rather than the exception. This chapter is an attempt to explore the consequences of this idea clinically and theoretically.

Psychoanalysis, throughout its history, has existed in a dialectical relationship with the norms of the middle classes of Western culture. On one hand, particularly at the beginning of its history, it played a subversive role. Sigmund Freud introduced into psychiatry an idea that was central to the romantic thinking of the 19th century. Ordinary life was more interesting, more conflictual, and darker in its texture than the normative life story of his times presumed: There was drama in everyday life, even though much of it was unconscious. During the oedipal phase, all of us were supposed to experience illicit desire, murderous impulses, and painful encounters with social limitations.

Nevertheless Freud also accepted the central tenets of the bourgeois conception of life. Civilized life confined these dramas to the unconscious. To work and to love was what human beings could expect at most. Only neurotic persons did not succeed in quite containing these dark undercurrents and therefore staged them, unwittingly, in their symptoms. For them, psychoanalysis could transform hysterical misery into ordinary unhappiness.

American ego psychology taught Americans that, underneath the neat picture of good people trying to make a life for themselves, the Freudian drama was still to be found. Nevertheless it accepted that making it financially and building a family were the primary goals in life. Hence, for decades, mental health was defined as a combination of autonomy and adaptation.

This goal came under fire from several camps during the 1960s and 1970s, when Western culture began to view fitting into bourgeois society as a goal that diminished human beings: psychoanalysis reacted to the changes in Western culture. The bourgeois ideal moved gradually away from successful adaptation and maintaining one's social status as a definition of the good life. Correspondingly, the ideal of the well-analyzed person was replaced by conceptions of human life more akin to the romantic view of human nature (Strenger 1989, 1997).

The 1950s brought new formulations and new goals. Humanistic psychology took self-actualization as the focal point of its image of human nature. In psychoanalysis, Winnicott (1960) spoke of the true self that expresses itself in the spontaneous gesture. Bollas (1989) made a valiant attempt to develop Winnicott's metaphor of the true self into one of much more depth and detail by speaking of elaborating the patient's personal idiom.

In France, adaptation was rejected by theorists of an existentialist bent. Lacan (1978) positively hated it. He saw ego psychology's emphasis on ego functioning as alienating the subject from itself. Normalization was not a goal he deemed worthy of a human life. Instead, he put aside the ideal of the subject capable of enunciating his desire and emphasized the tragic dimension of human existence.

In the United States, things changed as well. Heinz Kohut's (1977) self psychology integrated humanistic values of self-actualization into psychoanalysis. In many ways, the changes in American psychoanalysis reflected the values of liberal Baby

Boomers. Fitting in was not enough; finding one's "true voice" and relating authentically to others came to be central. A new generation of American analysts, mostly Ph.D.s influenced by the social and cultural changes of the 60s, repudiated adaptation as well.

At the center of much American theorizing is the capacity for intersubjective recognition. Relational psychoanalysts speak of the enrichment of the patient's subjectivity (Mitchell 1993) or even the capacity to live and enjoy the extremes of affective experience (Eigen 1998). Adaptation and normalization have come to seem flat as goals of analysis. A life worth living, it seems, cannot consist simply of making a success out of oneself—having a career, placing oneself in one of the more desirable slots professionally and financially, and having satisfying relationships simply do not do the job.

My question is, have the ideals of Western culture moved further once again, and does the formulation of "enrichment of subjectivity" or "developing personal idiom" capture what many people are looking for? This chapter is an attempt to explore a tendency of late-modern persons that is at once darker, more radical, and more exciting than these formulations imply. Sloterdijk (1996) and Gross (1999) claim that late-modern persons need to make contact with what Foucault (1984) called limit experiences: death, madness, unregulated sexuality, and encounters with the more dangerous edges of existence seem to have become a prerequisite for living a full life.

One could rightly argue that there have always been people who sought to go beyond such limits. Explorers, mountain climbers, sexual adventurers (once known as libertines), experimenters with drugs are not exactly new. Baudelaire and de Quincey wrote about drugs extensively in the 19th century. Giacomo Casanova filled 11 volumes with the stories of his sexual adventures. And from Columbus to Charles Lindbergh there were always those who risked their lives in adventurous conquests that put their lives at risk.

But in the bourgeois experience, the 19th- and the 20th-century experimentations with the self were considered extraordinary. More precisely, the bourgeois experience tended to relegate such experimentation to the fringes of society. On one hand, the category of the Bohemian that evolved in the

19th century provided the content for drama that the bourgeoisie loved to read about (Dumas's *La Dame des Camélias*) or hear and see on stage (Verdi's *La Traviata* moved many to tears). On the other hand, playing with limit experiences was preferably experienced through fictional accounts of others' lives. The bohème was also an object of envy; living at the edge was so much more interesting (and hence a preferred topic for literature) than the stifling life within the confines of respectability. Nevertheless, the goal of the bourgeoisie itself was to accept the discipline required to stay within these confines.

The hypothesis that I am exploring here is that something in the relationship of contemporary urban culture to experimentation with the self seems to have changed. The normative life narratives of vast strata of the urban middle classes in the Western world seem to create different relationships toward self-experimentation. Earlier conceptions saw the standard life trajectory as involving a moratorium that separated childhood from adulthood. Adolescence was the period in which young people were allowed (or even expected) to experiment a little bit in defining their own identity vis-à- vis their families. Then they were expected to find their place in society and embark on a course of life that was more or less predictable: marriage, family, career, followed by aging, retirement, and death.

There is evidence that this experimentation has become part of the normative life expectation in late modernity. The late-modern person is, to use the German philosopher Peter Sloterdijk's (1996) terms, involved in perpetual self-experimentation. A life lived without such experimentation is a life not truly lived. What was once the prerogative, both envied and admired, on one hand, and judged as marginal, on the other, has now become part of mainstream culture. Or, to be more precise, there is a variety of subcultures that sanctions various experimentations with the self that are accepted as legitimate parts of urban life.

Elsewhere (Strenger 1988) I have explored the idea that the pain of many people who turn to analytic help is that their sense of individuality is impaired. They desire to have a sense of authorship over their lives. They want to feel that they have shaped their lives according to their desires and that they have not been forced to live within limitations that they did not choose. It seems that this desire for authorship, for the sense of having created oneself freely, is becoming more prominent in contemporary urban culture.

Iris: In Search of the Right Style

When Iris came to see me the first time, she was 21 years old. She was a good-looking brunette of medium build who made a very serious impression. She was highly respectful and made every effort to be open and cooperative. She had attended some popular lecture of mine and hoped I would be able to help her.

Her problem? She had been involved for two years with a young man six years older than she. He was very smart and, in his opinion, right about pretty much everything. In particular, he had very clear views about what Iris's character flaws were, and he lectured her extensively on that subject. Iris had been trying desperately to please him; she felt that his criticism of her was justified, that she was not serious, dedicated, or focused enough. She was yearning for some warmth from him, but this seemed to be out of reach. At best there was some sex, but not enough of it either.

Iris was the daughter of Israeli parents who very much identified with the basic ethos of the country. Her father was hard working and single minded in his dedication to his job, which had brought the family economic success. Her mother was warm, but intent on her little comforts and not quite available. Iris had a brother eight years older than she who very much identified with his parents. His attitude toward Iris could be described as parental, and, from early on in her life, Iris was accustomed to lectures from both her father and her brother. Her mother generally tended to agree with them but did not interfere too much as long as no demands were made on her. The tenor of the lectures was that Iris had to be independent and hard working and should not expect others to shoulder the burdens of life for her.

Iris made the connections quickly: from an early age, Iris became accustomed to being in the position of the little girl lectured and admonished by men about her character flaws.

Her basic experience was that she never quite measured up to the standards that were applied to her, and her existential posture was that of straining to measure up to expectations. Her boyfriend effortlessly fitted into the mold her father and brother had created in her soul: it was enough for him to assume the posture of the knowledgeable critic to awaken in her the little girl who wanted to please and satisfy. For reasons of his own, he stuck to this role, and her biographical background made it easy for him to maintain it.

Within about half a year of our work together, Iris began to experience intense anger toward her parents and her boyfriend. She finally began to question the role she had been cast in: the little girl always falling short of expectations and eager to please knowledgeable men. She began to confront her boyfriend and question his authoritarian posture. At some point, she told him that, if he was not capable of a more egalitarian relationship, she would leave him. At first he reacted by trying to accommodate her, but it soon turned out that he seemed incapable of being in a relationship without having some type of power position.

After some painful confrontations and long deliberations, Iris came to the conclusion that she had no choice but to leave her boyfriend. After some months of mourning (she had loved him, despite his character flaws), she began to feel like a butterfly finally released from its cocoon. Her gait became more bouncing, her state of mind more cheerful. She was successful in the law studies she had embarked on, male students courted her, and she felt that our work was done. I felt that a significant piece of individuation had taken place and let her go with a warm handshake and best wishes for what was to come.

Three years after we had finished what turned out to be the first installment of her treatment, she called me for a consultation again. I opened the door—and was floored! In came a platinum blonde, dressed in tight jeans, her belly button pierced with a ring (you can deduce the length of her tank top). Her body was that of a typical aerobics teacher, and she had a perfect suntan to top it all off.

The first session, of course, was primarily an update. Iris had finished her law studies but had, for the time being, declined the offers she had received for internships. She could simply not imagine sitting in a law office 12 hours a day and then cramming for her bar exam. Her reluctance to continue her law career cut deeper than her reluctance to work 12-hour days. Iris had embarked on a quest that touched on the core of her identity. During the last year of her law studies she had embarked on two projects. First, she had enrolled in Tel Aviv's most prestigious course for bartenders. Second, she intended to be one of the most smashing bartenders in Tel Aviv. To do so, she began the process of giving her body the shape she wanted it to have.

At this point, some cultural explanation is in order. Bars in Israel, particularly in Tel Aviv, have a character very different from those in the United States and Britain. I have noticed that for many Americans the term bar has the association of lonely people getting drunk, and the bartender is thought of as being an understanding man or woman who both provides the liquor and caters to the need for a listening ear. Nothing could be further from the reality of Tel Aviv bars. Most of them are packed with young people, the erotic tension tangibly in the air. The atmosphere, however, is not that of an American singles' bar. Even though much of the action has to do with picking up and being picked up, there is something more fun loving and less desperate in the air than in a purely pickup place. The best of Tel Aviv's bars are places that celebrate life, beauty, and, of course, the endless variety of erotic experience.

This brings us to the center of the action: the bartender. Many bartenders in Tel Aviv, whether male or female, are stunningly good looking. Mostly in their 20s, many of them have perfectly shaped bodies, smooth movements. Their erotic auras are often a major constituent of the bar's ambiance. Female bartenders (and from now on I will speak only of them) are in many ways the queens of the night. They feel that, once behind the bar, they have a kingdom of their own. Caressed by the yearning eyes of the customers, they know that most of the males desire them. Few men will dare to make a pass because the competition is fierce. Those who do make passes too casually quickly learn that the bartender is a cut too high for them: they are brushed off like flies, with no more than a passing gaze telling them, "How did you even think you stood a chance?!"

The bartender is queen, because she is the one who can pick whom she wants. She is, in a sense, without competition. Most other women who sit at the bar are not physically at the center—and, even if the other women are attractive, the bartender is in the unique position of being the center of attention. She is in a position of power because in her official function she does not owe any of the men anything as a woman. Because the bartender can make such a huge difference in the atmosphere and success of a bar (many males will return time and again with the slight hope that this time they will be blessed by her grace), the owners of the place will pick the bartender carefully for looks, erotic aura, and power of personality. (It takes some strength to handle so much attention in the midst of the frenzy of doing the actual work.) Hence, getting the job at one of the more prestigious bars is a coveted goal for many young women in Tel Aviv; besides making good money, the very fact that they can say, "I work the bar at X," means that they belong to the select group of the beautiful people who attract the city's desire.

When Iris told me which bar she was working at, I could not help giving a whistle of appreciation. She took the compliment with style and pride.

What a transformation she had gone through! What a difference between the serious, subdued girl eager to please and give respect whom I had come to know almost four years earlier and the self-assured, beaming young woman who took off her shoes and tucked her legs under in the most relaxed of manners.

At first, there were some remnants of the past to be taken care of, though. It turned out that she had just ended a relationship that bore a remarkable resemblance to the one she had had with Isaac four years earlier. Ironically, it turned out, Jacob had even worked at the same company as Isaac for a while. The story had the distinct air of déjà vu. Jacob had the same style of condescending superiority and a slightly patronizing air. He was gifted, self-absorbed, and pretty sure that he was entitled to grading Iris's various personality traits. In a matter of three months' work we took up the themes of the first year of treatment for her to confront him. Soon she came to the conclusion that she had once again fallen into the same trap, and she decided to leave Jacob.

Soon after, Iris began to take full advantage of her new role of queen of the night. She was invited to a party, and she knew Jacob was going to be there. As she was now well entrenched in the web of bartenders in town, she sent out feelers and in no time was set up with a colleague, whom, for simplicity's sake, we shall call Adonis (and save ourselves the trouble of describing his looks). Adonis was fully informed that the evening was to be a settling of scores, and he was more than willing to play the role.

Iris, whose training at the gym had included quite a bit of jazz dance, soon took to the center of the dance floor and, with enthusiastic cooperation from Adonis, managed to transfix everybody's eyes on a performance of elegance and flowing eroticism. From the corner of her eye she made sure that Jacob (who was not bad looking, but did not begin to come close to Adonis) was suitably downtrodden and depressed. He left the party soon after. All it took for a perfect evening was that she and Adonis came to the conclusion that they had enjoyed their dancing enough to end the evening in bed, where Adonis turned out to have as much substance as his looks promised.

Iris was now at the center of Tel Aviv night life. Invited to the most coveted parties, surrounded by the protective cocoon of Adonises, she could take her erotic aura with her from the bar to the rest of town. Because it was so clear that she was in demand, she would at times chat up guys she was interested in from a position of strength. Her sex life was varied and enjoyable, her days spent primarily sleeping off the effects of long nights that included as much booze and nicotine as they included fun and sex.

Yet gradually something seemed not to be not quite right in this paradise of Tel Aviv nights. Some of the men she spent nights with actually turned out to be interesting; some even seemed to be decent human beings. And yet all of them disappeared pretty quickly–mostly after one night, sometimes after more. What the hell was wrong?

I began to wonder about the pattern of her sexual life. She enjoyed the sex itself, but did she really take the men to bed the first night for sheer pleasure? Or was there a deeper secret behind it? I thought that maybe she felt that, since she was so good looking, and since she was sure of her sexual abilities, she went for what she felt was the safest bet. Gradually a hypothesis emerged in my mind: maybe Iris's old fears of not being "good enough" had not really disappeared. Maybe Iris still feared that she was not sufficiently interesting, intelligent, and "developed." This fear had managed to disappear behind her success as a woman.

Yet, paradoxically, her strategy was backfiring. I had met this constellation with several patients before: beautiful young women who had problematic relationships with their fathers and who went to bed too soon out of fear that they would be dumped. Male psychology being what it is, the strategy tends to backfire: the women tend to be categorized as one-night stands, and the men never call again.

So, in an attack of therapeutic overzealousness, I tried to persuade Iris to accept a therapeutic contract that would oblige her not to go to bed with any man before she had met with him at least five times. I had used this therapeutic tactic in the past with several women patients caught up in similar dynamics. It had worked well for a simple reason: the patients found out that men would not run away even if they did not sleep with them right away. This discovery gave several women the chance to reconsider their self-image that they had nothing to offer but sex.

The session after I had tried to convince Iris of this idea, she sat down and, staring at me furiously, said, "I almost didn't come today. I was on the verge of sending you a check and telling you that the therapy was over. You completely fucked up last session. You didn't listen; you just expounded your theories to me and tried to pressure me into accepting your view of things."

Iris was both angry and hurt. It turned out that she had experienced my attempt to help her regain her self-esteem not as an attempt to help, but as a patronizing imposition of supposedly superior experience and knowledge. Fighting my instinct to defend myself, I tried to get it right this time. I listened and explored her experience of me. Gradually I realized that she had experienced me as not very different from Isaac, Jacob, and, ultimately, her father. I had become heir to a series of men whom she experienced as taking away her right to a mind and soul of her own.

Only after we had explored her experience in some depth and detail, did I tell her about my side of things. I acknowledged that, in that particular session, I had indeed been convinced that I knew exactly what was right for her. Even though my conscious intention had been therapeutic, I had obviously fallen into the trap of acting out a countertransference reaction. Once the therapeutic bond had been restored, I told her that, even though there was no doubt that I had made a mistake, there was something to be learned from it. We gradually gained more insight into the ways in which she had goaded me into the position where I became the caring, but all-too-knowing male who explained to her what was good for her.

Not surprisingly, this intersubjective exploration proved to be more fruitful than previous attempts at analyzing her pattern with men. Even though her relationship with me was very different in this second installment of our therapeutic work, there was still a subtext of my being the authoritative male whom she tried to please and impress.

It is intriguing that, throughout both installments of the therapy, there was no erotic dimension in the transference-countertransference, particularly given how much erotic experience was a major topic of our dialogue. I have wondered more than once whether I had a blind spot or whether Iris and I somehow colluded in avoiding the topic. I think that the explanation is different. The central issue that Iris brought to the therapy was not her sexuality. If anything, the erotic domain was one of the stages in which her search for recognition as an autonomous subject was played out in her life. The major transference issue centered on her search for recognition by male authority figures. In this respect, she exemplified Jessica Benjamin's (1989) idea that in male-dominated societies women feel that the father is the carrier of subjectivity, while the mother is experienced as not having full agency and subjectivity. The father becomes the representative of the external world, while the mother is a need-fulfilling object.

Iris's major developmental need was to be recognized as an autonomous, valuable subject and agent. My countertransference was, I believe, an attempt to meet this developmental need. The problem was that, by acting out the paternal role rather than investigating her need for this recognition, I fell into the trap of embodying the figure of authority that supposedly had the monopoly on recognition.

The turning point came when Iris broke out of this mold by angrily confronting me with my mistake. At that moment she ceased to put me in the position of sole holder of authority and established a position of mutuality. When I realized my mistake, accepted her criticism, and moved to a stance of joint exploration, we finally established a relationship of mutual recognition of like subjects (Benjamin 1995), which helped her to establish herself as an autonomous agent. Our dialogue became more open and also more humorous. As she now felt more at ease and less in need of being the good daughter who needed my approval, we could laugh at the ways we had both fallen into the trap that she had repeated so often in her life.

While something in her relations with men began to change at a deeper level, Iris still faced the question of how she wanted to live her life. She was less dependent than before on her new-found erotic power, and her use of this power was now more in the service of her true wishes and desires and less governed by her anxieties. Her dilemmas about how to live were not over. The opposite was true: on one hand, she was unsure that she wanted to continue the immersion in Tel Aviv's nightlife at the depth she was involved in now. She began to look into different kinds of jobs. It was also not clear that the alternative to working bars was to take the bar exam. It turned out that Iris's new-found self-confidence blended well with her intellectual abilities. Because of her intelligence, independence, and her ever-increasing ability to make open contact with people, she was even offered jobs in the new economy for which she had no experience.

It was at this point that she felt that she wanted to see how she was going to do on her own. I had to fight some of my paternal feelings. I felt that maybe I could help more. But this time, instead of letting the feelings take over, I discussed them with her. And the conclusion was that, even though there were so many open questions, Iris felt that she wanted to deal with them and was capable of doing so on her own.

Iris has since called me on the phone to give me an update. She has found a new direction that seems to integrate the various strands of her personality in a manner that is both personally satisfying and promising as a new career.

The Postmodern Body

Iris's search for self and identity had several layers. One of the main themes of our work has been described in the analytic literature from all possible angles: the process of individuating the self vis-à-vis parental introjects. Because this theme is well known, I will not dwell on it. The themes I want to focus on pertain to the desire for self-experimentation and self-creation that has become so ubiquitous in contemporary urban culture.

A caveat is in order. Large parts of the populations of both Western Europe and the United States adhere to more or less conservative life styles. What I am about to describe is typical of a particular stratum of large cities influenced by globalization; that is, it has moved beyond the West into cities like Tokyo. The culture I am about to describe is by no means marginal. As already mentioned, it includes professionals, some of whom occupy high-level positions, and it has moved beyond the confines of adolescent and postadolescent subgroups, even though it may be more pronounced in these age groups.

My surprise when I met Iris again three years after our first piece of work was immediate: she looked enormously different. There were the differences in details. Her workout regimen had changed her body. She had platinum blond hair. She had had her belly button pierced, and her clothing had changed dramatically. These changes of details added up to a change in the gestalt. From a serious "good girl," she had transformed herself into the epitome of the cool urbanite. She had worked out a new identity.

Let us put some of these changes into a wider cultural perspective. Iris's workout regimen may have been severe, but it is my impression that she was not untypical of many women and men of her generation. The proliferation of gyms in urban centers in the last few decades is enormous. Unlike the jogging culture of the 70s, gyms are not primarily about health. Their explicit goal is to shape the body. The contemporary gym is a sophisticated space designed to give its users the chance to sculpt their bodies (Gross 1999). Each machine indicates precisely which muscle group it develops. Personal trainers put together detailed programs that are designed to achieve the desired effect.

The gym culture is an industry that has achieved enormous proportions. It has assumed international brand names like Holmes Place, Studio B, Studio C, and the like, and it is equally geared to both genders. The theme that underlies this industry is the promise that you can get the body that you want. You are not fated to stay within the limits of what you were born with. The baseline of your genetically determined looks is just the basis on which you sculpt the desired result.

Sculpting the body has gone several steps further: every large or even medium-sized city in the Western world has plenty of shops that perform body piercing and tattoos. No longer are these shops hidden in seedy areas of town, nor is their clientele limited to marginal subcultures. Earrings for men long ago moved out of the subcultures of gays, punks, and the gothic life styles. Piercing of noses, eyebrows, belly buttons, vaginal lips, and so on has moved into social strata that even two decades ago would have recoiled from them: medical doctors, lawyers, and bankers can be found among the aficionados of these paraphernalia. Tattoos are no longer indicative of marginal identities but are to be found in all social strata. The extremes of body alteration have moved far beyond these boundaries. Subcultures like urban aborigines (Juno and Vale 1995), who go to often astonishing extremes in their body alterations, have defined identities, magazines, outlets, and gathering places. But the very fact that these subcultures have moved that much further shows how much mainstream, bourgeois culture has integrated its basics.

In the same manner, hair color has ceased to be "natural": the coloring of hair has, of course, been around for a long time. Mostly, though, coloring was used to hide the graying of hair. The current culture of hair coloring is very different—platinum blond, the color Iris chose—is indicative of the change: platinum blond does not imitate a natural hair hue. It explicitly states that it is a designer color. This statement holds even more true for various hues—ranging from purple and orange to greenish blue—that are not even close to any natural color. Hair, like the rest of the body, is the raw material for shaping the body as a work of art.

The Urban Self: The Desire for Experimentation

The postmodern body as the basis for alterations is the most tangible aspect of a much more pervasive theme. The urban self itself has become a potential work of art. Here, I believe, we are witnessing an interesting cultural shift. The 50s and 60s emphasized the need to find one's true self. Humanistic psychology spoke of self-realization. Winnicott's work focused on the idea of the true self, which was to be found behind the various layers of false selfhood.

Contemporary urban culture has become thoroughly Nietzschean. By saying so, I address one, albeit major, thread of Nietzsche's thought, his aestheticism and his view of self-creation as art, which has been highlighted by Alexander Nehamas (1985, ch 6). The cultural goal is no longer to find the true self hidden behind layers that have been imposed on us. True freedom consists in being able to shape oneself according to one's desire. For Nietzsche, the injunction "become who you are" did not mean to find a hidden, true self, but to shape consciously the materials of the self into an aesthetically compelling creation. Nietzsche's perspectivalism, of course, implied that there was no single model that could guide such self-creation. Nietzsche (1884, para 290), of course, was very conscious of the fact that such freedom was not unlimited. Hence he emphasized that self-creation needed merciless self-knowledge, insight into one's strengths and weaknesses. Otherwise, he argued, the creation would end up being both incoherent and tasteless. Successful self-creation is not indulging in the fantasy that you can be anything you like; it is to use the materials you have been given by nature by applying refined aesthetic sensibilities to create a self and a life that corresponds to your will.

One of the most important 20th-century theorists to continue Nietzsche's thought was Michel Foucault (1971). He rebelled against what he considered to be the tyranny of authenticity (1966). He explicitly defended the right of a person to build and play with his masks and identity. Unlike those who saw the persona, the false self, or any fixed social identity as an alienating construct that prevented the true, authentic self from unfolding, Foucault saw the possibility of shaping the self as a liberating possibility. In some of his last statements he explicitly referred to the self as something to be shaped like a work of art (1983).

As more conservative developmental and cultural schemata, Iris's experimentation with her self could easily be explained away as some adolescent attempt to define herself vis-à-vis her parents. I think that, in the current cultural context, this explanation would definitely miss the mark. Iris was considering who she wanted to be. The most obvious option for her would have been to continue the developmental line she had initiated. This would have meant doing her internship in a law firm and embarking on the type of life she had envisaged.

Yet I think that it would be simplistic to view Iris's dilemma as just the expression of a conflict between two competing identities. On a deeper level, Iris needed to feel that she had really chosen and shaped her identity. One might argue that identities are not chosen but are grown into, that they are defined by the basic constituents of one's existence. Yet, according to the working hypothesis explored here, the basic assumption of contemporary urban culture is that identity is created, not found.

Iris needed to feel that it was within her power to create an identity that, for most of her life, had seemed out of reach for her. After a lifetime of trying to please men, she now was in the position of meeting them on the battleground of the war between the sexes– and to do so from a position of power. Yet I do not think that Iris's choice was primarily motivated by her past. She was thrilled that she could choose to be who she wanted to be. She had never doubted her intelligence, and it was clear to her that she could make her way up the ladder of bourgeois success. She had stamina; she knew how to invest herself in serious tasks.

There was, however, an aspect of urban life that had always seemed to be out of reach for her. In the past, when she went out with friends, it had always seemed to her that the party was going on elsewhere: there were the beautiful, easygoing kings and queens of the sexual arena, those who moved around with the assurance that they were going to be the center of attention, that their sheer attractiveness would give them a place of distinction. They were the rulers of the nightlife. Deep inside,

Iris had always felt that the hard workers of the law faculty were trying to make up with hard work what they believed they could not obtain otherwise—desirability and status.

Her life had been geared toward her being the serious girl that her parents had wanted her to be. But her secret desire had always been to belong to the club of those who attain their place in society by the sheer animal magnetism of their attractiveness. Iris's project, therefore, became to shape herself in the image of the fantasy that she had harbored secretly for many years. She wanted truly to become the author of her own self, to transcend what had seemed unbridgeable limitations. People like her and her family were not cut out to belong to the club of the truly desirable. She had always felt that the severe standards of quality and independence with which she had been imbued by her family were a compensation for this lack of desirability.

I do not mean to say that Iris simply realized an old fantasy. It seems to me that her deepest desire was to feel that she was truly free to choose who she was going to be. The limitations of her upbringing were to be transcended. It was unbearable for her never to know what it was like to be someone who was very different from what she had known up to that point in her life.

Toward the end of the second installment of our work, when Iris began to reconsider her career options, she could do so from a position of choice. Now she did not go for achievement because of a lack of alternatives, but because she was someone who knew that she could choose to be who she wanted. This new stance, however, in turn created many quandaries. What were her priorities going to be? What was really important for her? Which identity would she want to adopt? Was it possible to unite components of her identity as cool urbanite bartender with the demands of working in a high-tech company? Iris was willing to accept these problems. She preferred to live with the complexity of choice than with the sense of limitation. In other words, she preferred the complexities imposed on her by her newly gained sense of authorship to the sense of fatedness (Strenger 1998) that had governed her life before.

From a feminist point of view, the question might arise whether Iris indeed increased her sense of authorship or whether she just fell prey to the pressures of an anorectic culture and turned herself into an object of male desire. The success of the treatment, it might be argued, was that she could find a more authentic voice by ridding herself of the introject of male authority that defined her worth. But, instead, the argument might run, she turned men into the source of her worth by making herself into the epitome of what men desire. Although I might agree with some of that reasoning (and some of my interventions were guided by similar thoughts), I feel that Iris's project to find her own style, mentally and physically, was an expression of her desire for a sense of authorship. Authorship entails the shaping of the self according to one's desire. This Nietzschean motif of self-creation, as Foucault (1971) was at pains to point out, may often conflict with the need to fit in, to have close, stable relationships, and to have serenity of mind. My experiences in the consulting room reflect the impression generated by looking at contemporary urban culture at large; an ever-growing number of people see the possibility of experimenting with themselves as essential to the good life.

As to Iris's investment in becoming the embodiment of the cool urbanite woman, it is tempting to reduce this to the need to be worthy of love, which may, to some extent, be true. Iris and I talked about this motif. Nevertheless, I believe that such an explanation can be reductive. I believe that it is unwise to pathologize a desire that is as ubiquitous as the wish to be the object of desire. For too many years it has been a simple tenet of much analytic theorizing that this desire is simply the expression of female narcissism. Wanting to be an object of desire is one of the central needs of human beings—both female and male (only antiquated conceptions of masculinity would classify this desire as necessarily homosexual). Shaping one's body in the image of what one's culture deems to be desirable is as powerful a motivator as any other.

True, this desire has cruel implications. The horrendous competition for the gaze of the other (or the same) sex is fraught with tension and anxiety. Age becomes a tragedy rather than a natural part of life, because in present-day culture the ideal body is postadolescent. And most of us, notwithstanding the amount of time we spend at the gym, will never get anywhere close to the ideal of the supermodel, the aerobics teacher, or the body builder. I was, in fact, quite happy for Iris when she cut down on her workout regimen and became a little less concerned about the precise shape of her abdominals. I did not take her preoccupation with her body to be pathological. It just seemed that, in the total balance of her life, the amount of anxiety involved in every change in her body shape was taking too much of a toll.

It could be argued that the urban culture I am describing has put power rather than love into the center of human existence. This may be true particularly for the growing singles' culture that makes up a large part of the population, particularly of large Western European cities. Games of desirability often take up a large portion of single life, as mercilessly depicted in Candace Bushnell's (1996) *Sex in the City*.

It may not be coincidental that the successful HBO television series of the same name has softened Bushnell's dark emphasis on the importance of power in New York's single scene. This change is, I believe, only partially to be accounted for by considerations of ratings. The series puts more emphasis on yearning for love hidden behind the sophisticated courting games of the city. This yearning has, of course, not disappeared. As we saw, Iris yearned for love–but she needed to be able to meet men on terms that corresponded to her deep-seated desire for an existential sense that she had full authorship of her identity.

FINAL REFLECTIONS

At the beginning of this chapter I briefly pointed out the dialectical relationship between psychoanalysis and dominant cultural paradigms of its environment. My starting point was Sloterdijik's (1996) thesis that urban Western culture has turned self-experimentation into a central tenet of its ethos. This ethos of self-experimentation and self-creation creates a fascinating social reality: people may have more freedom than ever before to shape themselves. There are more life styles, cultures and subcultures, beliefs and preferences to choose from than ever before.

The consequences are highly complex, though. In large European cities the number of people living on their own has skyrocketed: the number ranges from 27% to over 50%, depending on the country (*Time Out* 2001). Singlehood and serial monogamy have become legitimate life choices. One of the unavoidable side effects of the preponderance of singlehood is that the population of most Western European countries is decreasing, creating the need to import foreigners to keep the economy going.

It could easily be argued that the culture of self-experimentation, if taken to its extreme, makes long-term commitments and raising children nearly impossible. This ethos, if indeed it becomes a significant element in Western culture, could self-destruct. A person's concern with exploring endless possibilities, various careers, and different life styles may lead to the point where this culture falls back into itself like a black hole (Fukuyama 1999).

These trends have a frightening impact if viewed from the standpoint of public policy, demography, and sociology. They are haunting philosophically. And they create interesting quandaries for the practicing clinicians whose commitment is not to the general population or the survival of Western culture but to the search of an individual patient's search for a good and fulfilling life.

In the age of self-experimentation, this search may lead to different types of limit experiences. Iris's exploration led to immersion in the panerotic sphere of Tel Aviv nightlife. Elsewhere (Strenger 1998, ch 1) I have recounted the story of my encounter with a woman who was involved in heavy S&M. In many other cases, the use of drugs like marijuana and Ecstasy has become normative in large Western cities.

Respect for a patient's subjectivity and autonomy prevents us from simply disqualifying the quest for authorship over one's identity as pathological. Such pathologization would be no more legitimate than would be the imposition of Western values on non-Western societies, particularly as subcultural phenomena like S&M, rave parties, and body alterations have acquired massive followings throughout the Western urban culture.

In the last two decades, psychoanalysis has largely come to distrust its own inclination to make itself into the arbiter of what is healthy and wholesome and what is pathological and needs to be cured. If, as Adam Phillips (1995) has argued, psychoanalysis is about helping people to be more interesting to themselves, our position becomes more complex. We may certainly engage a patient to reflect on the values of the culture that guides her life choices. We need not endorse these values and life styles just because the patient identifies with them. I did not hesitate to invite Iris to reflect on the extremes to which she had gone to keep her body in perfect shape. But I refrained from simply passing judgment on them. Iris did not have a disorder belonging to a nosological category like anorexia or bulimia, which would have legitimized my taking an authoritative stance. She derived much pleasure from her mode of life, even if it entailed some suffering

The Nietzschean (1884) strand of contemporary Western urban culture raises issues that are not easy to confront. The view of life as a work of art to be lived in the richest and most fulfilling manner raises powerful questions about the language of pathology and health that has governed psychoanalysis for most of its existence. Patients like Iris are not an exception in the private practices. A rather large percentage of patients do not come to treatment because they have any of the classical symptoms. Many do not have any syndrome classified in the DSM, and even if they do, these symptoms are often epiphenomenal to an existential dynamics.

One might still argue that a lack of overt pathology does not mean that there is no pathology on a deeper, dynamic level. It is tempting to follow authors like Chasseguet-Smirgel (1984), who argue that individuals as well as and cultures that do not respect the traditionally defined differences between the generations and sexes are essentially perverse and thus pathological. I believe that such a sweeping denunciation is both intellectually and ethically problematic. In my clinical judgment Iris and many other patients of her generation with whom I have worked are essentially healthy. They face deep existential conundrums that are generated by the space of freedom of contemporary urban culture.

On this issue I side with the position Stoller took in his later years. After decades of investigation he came to reject the idea that there is an essential psychodynamic difference between what is considered "normal" and "perverse" sexuality. Furthermore his investigations of the porn industry (Stoller 1991a) and the world of professional S&M (Stoller 1991b) led him to the conclusion that the members of these cultures are no more pathological than people who adhere to more traditional lifestyles.

It is easy to forget how much straightforward suffering and renunciation can often be associated with such traditional life styles. As Nancy Chodorow (1994) has poignantly shown, growing into "standard" heterosexuality involves a great deal of compromise formation. She presents a powerful argument that this "standard" heterosexuality is more of a cultural construct than a natural given, and believes that this construct often functions as a straightjacket that precludes people from finding their individual sexual voice and identity.

I therefore believe that both wholesale pathologization and thoughtless celebration of the urban culture of self-experimentations are to be avoided. As I have shown elsewhere (Strenger 2002a), the culture of self-experimentation can in many ways be seen as the logical extreme of the liberation movement of the 1960s and 1970s. For many of us, the result may not be what we hoped for. Yet, for the time being, careful investigation of the consequences of this development seems more fruitful to me than either endorsing or condemning it.

Sociologist Anthony Giddens (1992) has argued that the most prominent characteristic of late modernity is hyperreflexivity. Choices are made not on the basis of traditional values and criteria, but on the basis of the reflexive process of individual deliberation. Hyperreflexivity is the ultimate expression of Western liberalism, and thus maximizes personal freedom. It also imposes great responsibility on the individual, as all choices are supposed to reflect one's character and personality rather than traditional structures.

In contemporary Western culture, the desire for a distinct sense of individuality is experienced by many persons as a fundamental existential need. As I have tried to show (Strenger 1998), the existential dynamics of many patients are governed by their profound need for a sense of authorship over their lives. By authorship I refer to the subjective experience that one has shaped one's life actively according to one's desire and personal preference and what could be called one's aesthetic of existence (Foucault 1984; Bollas 1989; Eigen 1998). This is the person's sense of what type of life is worth living for her, what dimensions of life she experiences as central to a fulfilled life.

Iris's story shows these dynamics in detail. Her need to try out various identities shows the late-modern need to be sure that the self has been shaped autonomously. The point is that many people do not have a well-established aesthetics of existence. I believe that an important aspect of what many people search for in therapy is assistance in consolidating their aesthetics of existence. This can be expressed in a conflict among different life styles that seem attractive, interesting, and fulfilling. These people need to sort out their hierarchy of goals (Gedo 1979) and create a gestalt of what they want their lives to be.

The point is that human beings cannot make such choices in a vacuum. As I have tried to show in detail (Strenger 1998), the human search for authorship is poignant because none of us chooses the base materials of our lives: not parents, body, gender, innate talents, native language and culture, nor any of the other basic materials are chosen: they are given to us. We are like bricoleurs, who have to work with *objets trouvés* in a junkyard rather than choosing the base materials of ourselves in advance. This is exactly what Nietzsche (1884, para 290) meant when he said that the art of living is characterized by giving style to one's character, and that this necessitates a clear vision of one's strengths and weaknesses. Choosing a way of life and consolidating a personal aesthetics of existence was once the prerogative of a few. Now it has become an integral part of late modern urban culture, and psychoanalysis needs to find a vocabulary to address this theme.

Chapter 2

Nobrow: Forming an Identity In Urban Culture

The Difficulties of Forming an Identity in the Global Village

In this chapter I examine the immense impact of the new economy on cultural standards. The patient, whom I call Ben, exemplifies a constellation that I believe to be prevalent. His parents were part of a social and moral order based on clear hierarchies: people with academic degrees and respectable professions were more valuable and more entitled to respect than those who did not have such a background. Professions that required high standards of ethical integrity provided social status that was often not commensurate with their income. Ben's problem was a function of the clash between the social and cultural standards of his parents and those of his own generation.

This chapter also reflects a personal process I am undergoing. My own cultural universe is defined in conservative terms. I grew up in a culture that emphasized continuity, the hierarchy of high culture versus low culture. My training was based on immersion in complex texts and contexts and on studying intellectual developments ranging over centuries, and sometimes millennia. For a long time, it was clear to me that there was a canon of works that provided the purest exemplification of the human spirit at its best.

In my experience, the encounter with Generation X (for sociological definitions see Thau and Heflin 1997), particularly with its younger members, forces me to struggle with many of the assumptions about what constitutes a valuable life. My conclusions are, of necessity, tentative. I am arguing primarily that the processes of identity formation of GenXers are profoundly shaped by the lack of cultural continuity between them and their parents.

SOME CHARACTERISTICS OF GENERATION X: THE IMPACT OF THE NEW ECONOMY

It is almost a platitude to say that historical time has sped up. Within one generation's time, we have witnessed a radical change in the global political and social order. Social and political theorists (Fukuyama 1999; Huntington 1999; Friedman 2000; Frum 2000) are still trying to figure out what the new global order is, while a whole generation is being shaped by this new reality.

The Reagan-Thatcher era of the 80s created a climate epitomized by movies like *Wall Street* and novels like *American Psycho.* Deregulation of the financial sector created a dizzying new economic reality. Using novel financial instruments, people could buy and sell huge corporations and reap billions (Ehrlich and Rehfeld 1989). Financial whiz kids barely 25 years old commanded salaries measured in seven digits on Wall Street just because of their ability to detect minute fluctuations in the market and capitalize on them with split-second decisions.

The news of the 80s was generated by great financial manipulators. Investment banking was where the action was. It turned out that the huge organizations that had provided the 50s and 60s with their economic and social hierarchies, infrastructures–the corporations that seemed to become as much a frame of reference as nation states–were vulnerable to the manipulation of small numbers of individuals who could buy these organizations, tear them apart, sell their assets, merge them with others, and scale them down at will.

The geniuses of the age were people like Michael Milken, whose pushing of the junk-bond market created the possibility of gifted and gutsy speculators to tackle the largest companies in leveraged buyouts. Milken got to the point where his very signature as underwriter of a bond issue was worth 2.5 million dollars.

Of course. there were backlashes. Those excluded from the vertiginous ascent to wealth of the financial wizards felt deep satisfaction when Milken and others, like Boesky, went to prison. Movies like *Wall Street* extolled the virtues of decent, hard-working folks (played by Martin Sheen) and vilified the amoral belief in greed and power of the new players on the financial market (played by Michael Douglas).

But the new social reality was a fact: you could be a millionaire by age 25 if you had the knack of making the right split-second decisions–buying or selling hundreds of millions of dollars of stocks and bonds at the right moment. You could have a two million dollar penthouse outfitted by the latest rage of designers if you worked in a legal firm specializing in mergers and acquisitions.

Anyone who held on to the idea of having a job in a large corporation and gradually climbing up the corporate ladder did not understand the rules of the new game. You had to be on the list of headhunters who would rush you from one job to the next at least once a year or so. This process sped up the move through the various income brackets. Those who stuck to outdated notions of loyalty to a company were likely to end up on the sidelines. Companies were not benevolent mothers who nursed you and your family from cradle to grave; they were commodities to be bought, sold, merged, stripped of their assets. The question was whether you were going to be among the predators or the passive victims that were eaten up.

The 80s saw a new category, the Yuppie–a category charged with ambivalences. On one hand, the term was generally used with some disdain; Yuppies were supposed to be self-centered to the point of emotional autism. Instead of caring about rebellion against the system and striving for social justice, as their Baby-Boomer predecessors had done in the 60s and early 70s, they cared only for Porsches, Rolex watches, Armani suits, and expense accounts.

The 1990s, after a brief recession, saw the crumbling of the political order of post-World War II. Political certainties like the Cold War, which maintained the power balance of the world, vanished literally within one year, leaving after them a reality that experts and politicians alike are still trying to decode (Fukuyama 1999; Huntington 1999).

At the same time, the new information technologies created a world radically different from that which humanity had ever known. The metaphor of the global village has become a concrete, lived reality. Software projects are run around the clock by teams living in opposite time zones. Corporations have become truly global because there is no need to have management, production, and marketing in the same areas (Friedman 1999).

The financial success stories of the 80s were dwarfed by what the 90s brought: a single man, Bill Gates, amassed a fortune exceeding the GDP of many countries. Entrepreneurs in their 20s came up with ideas that within three years created fortunes measured in hundreds of millions of dollars. For the first time, the flow of capital was truly democratized: you needed no social connections anymore to get access to great amounts of money that would allow you to make even greater amounts later on.

One of the most tangible pressures created by the new economy was a tightening of stress on those in their 30s. If they hadn't landed a job in one of the fast-track areas and placed themselves in the "promising upstart category" by 30, they likely would be left out. If they had not placed themselves in the niche that catered to the new economy, they would end up doing the trivial, boring work that is left to those who do not have the knack of fitting themselves into the high-speed train to early riches.

This economic buildup also reversed hierarchies that seemed immutable for a long time: careers in once-respected professions like medicine became unattractive. Why waste your time acquiring a profession in which you start making money at an age when others already have their first ten million invested in mutual funds and venture capital? In fact, many physicians turn their careers around by abandoning medical practice and joining startups in the exploding biotech market, or they are developing software products for the profession they thought they would themselves practice.

Generation Xers, particularly the gifted ones, enjoy a freedom unknown to earlier generations of the 20th century. For them it is a matter of course that gender and sexual orientation are constructions, and that each individual can create the particular configuration (I am deliberately using this term from computer lingo) that suits her or him.

The professional possibilities open to GenXers are more varied than those of any other society we have ever known. They feel that there is very little wisdom of earlier generations that they can use to navigate their way in a world that simply outpaces that wisdom. The openness of their lived reality is achieved at a price: the complexity of their path to an established identity is greater than it was in more strictly structured societies.

In other words, many members of Generation X do not see as an alluring possibility the prospect of maturing into a profession and gradually attaining social status and a sense of achievement. The meritocratic democratization of the accessibility of capital has created the opposite effect (Holtz 1995; Thau and Heflin 1997). One of the most fascinating implications of the new economy is that many of the new functions are, as yet, not even defined as professions by the established academic orders, and that new roles and professions arise that do not even have a name. We see some of the implications of this process later in the case presentation.

NOBROW CULTURE

Another factor that shaped the new generation's mental images is the radical subversion of the dichotomy between high culture and popular culture that was a matter of course for previous generations.

The humanistic tradition that emerged in the Renaissance created the idea of a cultural canon that had to be mastered if truly cultivated minds were to be inspired (Bloom 1987). The canon in question changed over time, but the idea that there are masterpieces of (presumably Western) literature, philosophy, plastic arts, and music that define true culture remained relatively unquestioned well into the 1960s.

It was taken for granted that there is a profound qualitative difference between deep, real, high culture and shallow culture, which has only entertainment value. The emergence of electronic mass media and the entertainment industry only deepened this conviction: cultural commentators from T. S. Eliot (1975) to Allan Bloom (1987) felt that high culture had to fortify its trenches if it was to preserve the heritage that defined what the West stood for.

The turnaround of the 1960s and 70s has been discussed in hundreds of books: Andy Warhol's dictum "art is what you can get away with" marked the beginning of an era that undermined distinctions that had been taken for granted (Kimball 1999).

The 1980s and 90s brought the reshuffling of categories to new heights. The diminishing willingness of states to finance high culture made it necessary to package culture in marketable ways. A telling example is the show that united the three most famous tenors of the 70s and 80s, Luciano Pavarotti, Placido Domingo, and José Carreras into a unit called "The Three Tenors." A potpourri of operatic arias, popular tunes. and operettas was interspersed with moments in which all three tenors screamed high C's into microphones that fed sound systems blasting to huge audiences. Those of us who had experienced opera as high culture could only react with shock to the resulting hodge- podge.

David Seabrook (2000) has dubbed the culture that has emerged from the eradication of the distinction between highbrow and lowbrow culture *Nobrow*. Seabrook's main argument is that marketing has permeated the production of culture to the point where distinctions of quality have been superseded completely by the marketing of cultural products.

The frame of reference of Generations X and Y seems to be much more horizontal than vertical. Books have been around for millennia, and the cultural foundations of earlier generations were codified in them. The medium that is most characteristic for Generations X and Y is the Internet, which, as a global phenomenon, is little more than a decade old. Hence these generations feel much more defined by their relations with their contemporaries than by their dependence on the past (Holtz 1995).

They are creating a cultural space that is detached from earlier cultural forms. They have developed a language that is hardly intelligible to those foreign to the scene of rave parties, the cultural space of chill-out rooms, after parties, and the like. Their consistent use of grass, Ecstasy, and other drugs has evolved into a subculture barely accessible to earlier generations, which still experience drug use as an emancipatory act of subversive nature.

During the same time period, academia went through a similar upheaval. The canon of Western culture was attacked as nothing but a reflection of Western, phallocentric imperialism. The canon was, so it was said, just a collection of dead white males. Courses on cultures that had been excluded from the canon began to be seen as no less valuable than those which taught the purportedly immutable canon of Great Books.

The interpretation of these changes splits commentators into two bitterly opposed camps: neoconservatives, like Bloom (1987), Kimball (1999), and Himmelfarb (1999), feel that the edifice of Western culture is falling apart; others, like Paglia (1990), see the dissolution of the canon as a blessing. Finally there are those like Martha Nussbaum (1997), a renowned philosopher and legal and classical scholar, who try to find a middle ground in the war between those who decry and those who celebrate Nobrow culture.

As I mentioned at the beginning of this chapter, I have trouble making up my mind. Emotionally I often vacillate between a sense of loss and the exhilaration of watching the emergence of something completely new (Beaudoin 1998). Yet, as a clinician, I am faced with the task of understanding members of Generation X who have grown into the Nobrow culture. And, as it turns out, it takes some effort to be able to understand them on their own terms–and thus to be helpful.

BEN: "I HAVE NO FOUNDATION"

The young man in my office was edgy, nervous, fidgety. "I don't believe in shrinks. I really don't," he said. "But if you helped X (a friend of his who had been in therapy with me), maybe you can help me. I don't think, though, at all that my problem is psychological. My problem is *real,* man. Just fucking real. I have only one problem: I have no academic background. I have no basis whatsoever for what I do. OK. I'm this big success story; but it's going to break down *sometime!* I'm a fake, and one day they'll know it."

Here is Ben's story. At age 21, Ben joined a startup company that developed computer games. He was surrounded by engineers, people with MBAs, people with degrees in art and graphic design. "You understand? They all know something.

They have an education. And they know what they know. Here I come in, knowing nothing, sitting in those meetings, and suddenly I begin to pour out ideas that combine everything with everything. I come up with ideas for new products, and they invest 100,000 bucks in a pilot after a few minutes of discussion!"

Ben was now 27 years old. The startup had become a well-known company that made a lot of money. "And I'm the number three of the fucking place. This is ridiculous. I'm called creative director. They had to come up with some bloody name for something that doesn't exist. Well, Doctor, what are you gonna do about *that?*"

I am on a first-name basis with my patients (as is usual in Israel), and Ben usually called me by my first name. Whenever he called me "Doctor," I felt simultaneously amused and annoyed. Ben used this term to express something that combined a challenge, an implicit devaluation of who I was and what I did, and a sly curiosity about how I was going to handle the situation.

For the first half year or so, the sessions were not easy for me at all. Ben had several offputting habits. He constantly wriggled around in the chair, moved up and down, went into prolonged sessions of scratching his hair violently and compulsively, then played around with the armrest of his chair. His tension, irritation, subliminal rage, and physical discomfort were contagious; I would sometimes feel like climbing up the wall. It is not easy to handle those situations; telling a patient that his physical presence is irritating and offputting may be experienced by him as a rejection and make further work impossible. It was to take me quite some time to figure out how to handle all this.

I gradually tried to get a sense of Ben's biography. Ben was the first-born son of a father who was a respected academic. "He's this really respected man. Everybody wants his advice. He's an excellent, methodical teacher. Does his research very thoroughly. And he never made any money. Just the bloody salary from the university."

"Oops," I thought, "There we go: the father who is a modest academic, thorough, well read, but making no money. And there goes Ben, 27 years old, already making a pile of money and with stock options waiting that will turn him into a millionaire soon. That's a reasonable ground for developing a sense of guilt. In addition. it could explain why he feels he is a fake without foundations."

I tried, time and again, to get Ben to talk about his past. But all I got in reply was, "Doctor, leave me alone, will you? I couldn't care less about your theories that childhood makes people this way or that way. My parents were really OK. Warm, supportive. OK? I couldn't talk about my sex life. But it wasn't so bad. They knew I fucked around a lot, and they weren't thrilled, but they were fine. You're barking up the wrong tree, Doctor, and you're not helping me a bit."

I grew desperate. Somehow I could not get a handle on this case. Whatever I tried did not work. Sometimes I thought that Ben was subtly devaluating me as a representative of high culture. If he felt so worthless compared with people like his father, this might be a way of venting his rage. His derogatory use of "Doctor," his constant reminders that he was investing time and money but did not get anything in return were marvelous ways to finish an issue that had been bugging him throughout life.

My efforts to work with Ben on this issue were about as helpful as sugar pills. We were, I had to admit, stuck.

Then came the day when I had a sore throat. I kept some lozenges on the table and took one every now and then to stop my cough. Ben, as usual fidgeting around in his chair and scratching his head, suddenly moved over, took one of the lozenges, and said, "You certainly don't mind." And he stuffed it into his mouth.

I felt paralyzed. Saying no would make me look stingy. Expressing my anger was not good therapeutic etiquette. Ben continued to drone on about how horrible it was to be a success story without foundations or credentials; how frightening it was to be all over the papers as one of the *Wunderkinder* of the Israeli high-tech industry knowing that he was a fake. And I sat in my chair, paralyzed and completely *livid.*

At some point I decided that if I was not going to talk with Ben about this I was either going to be completely inefficient, because I could not get my mind off it, or I would, at some point, act out my anger—which was not going to make me any more efficient.

So I said, "Ben, let's talk about the lozenge." He, with his usual mischievous smile, said, "Yes, what about it?"

I answered, "Wouldn't you want to think about what happened?" I hated myself. I sounded exactly like the stereotype of a shrink, I was so bloody *stilted!* No wonder—I really felt like hitting him and kicking him out of my office. The lozenge was just the proverbial drop that made the barrel spill over. For half a year I had felt that he was going to damage the armchair he was sitting on. For half a year I had to clean off the dandruff that he left on the chair with his eternal headscratching. For half a year he would intrude into my space physically by sliding down in his chair and stretching his legs in a way that made sure we were going to get in each other's way.

"Oh, I see," he said. "Now we are going to talk about our relationship. That's one of the things you shrinks really love to do, don't you? Well, about the lozenges. They were on the table. I asked you whether I could have one, then I took one and put it into my mouth. I felt like having one. I also have a bit of a sore throat, so they come really handy. That's all there is. What is your analysis, Doctor?"

I still tried not to go through the roof and ended up saying something appropriate to a kindergartener: "You didn't ask me if you could have a lozenge. You told me that I didn't mind, and you took one." He smiled at me, and his facial expression was something like, "Yup, Doctor. So your wisdom boils down to the depth of whether I *asked* for the lozenge or not."

Finally, I blew my top! "Look, Ben," I said, "The lozenge is really the tip of the iceberg. I've been sitting with you in this room for more than half a year, really making an effort to be helpful. What I get in return is disdain, devaluation, all kinds of little infringements on my physical and mental territory. I have tried to find out with you why you are so fidgety and restless. I have tried to indicate to you that your physical behavior is something worth understanding. Your reaction was mostly this grin that says, 'Oh, do cut the shrink bullshit, will you?' "

I continued, "So now I will oblige you and cut the shrink bullshit and just tell you what I feel. It's a fucking nightmare to sit with you. Your behavior makes me feel incredibly uncomfortable. You have no sense of propriety, no respect for my physical and mental boundaries. I have no intention of cleaning your dandruff off my leather chairs. I don't care whether you think that I'm a bourgeois shmuck who cares about nothing but his nice furniture. From now on, I expect you to behave like a *mensch*. Just the basics, OK? Like respecting that you are a guest in my consulting room. Like stopping your bloody tendency to insinuate constantly that what I do for a living is a stupid charade. You're here to get help. So, if you want any help, you better start behaving in a way that makes help possible—and some basic politeness hasn't harmed anybody either!"

He looked flabbergasted but quickly regained his usual composure (or discomposure) and said with mock empathy, "You must really be suffering!"

I retorted, in the same angry tone, "Don't give me your arrogant smile again. I have no intention of putting up with it. Yup, I am *not* enjoying myself. I also feel like shit for the way I'm blowing off steam, but I guess you've been working hard to get me to this moment!"

Now, really taken aback, he looked like a child who had just received a huge morality talk from his father. I said, "Look, Ben, I'm sorry that it had to come out this way, but maybe now you'll find it less ridiculous to think with me about why you make it impossible to be in the same room with you. I mean, it's absurd: you suffer, you need help, and you really do everything to make it impossible to help you."

My blowup did get to Ben. It began to cross his mind that I was not some impersonal, untouchable authority protected by the knowledge from the book-lined walls around his armchair. But he was, for all intents and purposes, still desperate; he still felt a cheat, a fraud, and devoid of foundations. He was still enormously restless.

But now we actually began to talk. It was not just Ben who had changed. I had changed, too. I had come to accept that my relatively laid-back style of work, my attempts to induce an analytic process of self-reflection, affective crystallization, intersubjective elucidation, and historical reconstruction simply were not helpful to Ben.

So what did he need? Often he needed advice, or at least active help in thinking through his next steps. Like most high-tech startups, the company he worked with was quite a mess. Mark, the founder and CEO, was a man with good hunches, an uncanny intuition for where the market was going, and a knack for negotiating deals. But he had neither the inclination to invest time in developing the company's organizational structure nor the talent needed to do so.

Mark's management skills were minimal. He made up for this lack by creating strong emotional ties with his employees and manipulating them by implying, "How can you do this to me after all I've done for you?" Ben was particularly vulnerable to this type of manipulation. He felt that he had been given his position without having earned it. After all. he had no foundations.

One of the interesting, and weird, aspects of Ben's situation was that, after three years with the company, he had no written contract. He was being paid nicely, but none of his rights, including the all-important stock options, had been formalized by contract. Not having a contract greatly contributed to Ben's sense of insecurity: didn't it mean that his position, his income, and his earnings depended on the love, or liking, and the whims of one man, who could withdraw them at any time? And didn't it mean that maybe he didn't get a contract precisely because he really wasn't there by merit?

First I tried to work with him on why he would not press the issue of a contract. At some point ("Doctor, why don't you stop the shrinking? What do you think I should do?") I simply began to act as a consultant. The result was, "Doctor, you've never been as useful as today!"

Ben had trouble with his girlfriend, too. He often did not feel like sleeping with her, whereas he was crazily attracted to other women and was on the way to falling in love with one of the many media stars he kept meeting at parties. Again, my attempts to deal with this situation analytically were of no use. At one point, I casually mentioned to Ben one of the basic truths (one might say, truisms) of existential philosophy: "You know, it's one of the persistent illusions in life that we can get all the goodies, but it turns out that choices always have a price. And there is no such thing as not choosing." Ben was astonished. The idea of paying a price was completely alien to the "I want it all, and I want it now!!!" culture he lived in.

Time and again we returned to his sense of being a fraud. Sometimes I would talk sociology with him: "There is no name for what you do, because what you do has come into existence only in recent years. And in the total mess of your company, there are no clearly defined roles anyway." Ben was ideas factory, project coordinator, consultant-for-all-times-and-topics. Surprisingly, he was called "the company's Valium." Yes, the very same Ben who drove me crazy with his restlessness turned out to thrive under pressure. When everything was falling apart, he was the man everybody turned to. He stabilized situations, gave everybody (including his boss) clear-cut instructions about what to do and say. His cool authority made everybody feel safe. He would make decisions, and large sums were invested along the lines of ideas that just seemed to pop up in his mind.

We spoke of the structure of his talents. He had an uncanny sense for visual concepts, the knack of sensing what was going to be "in" with Generation Y (the main clientele for the company's products), an intuitive grasp of how to organize teams around tasks that were only vaguely defined, and the innate authority of those endowed with leadership qualities. He was the quintessential hot shot of the new economy.

"But I don't have a degree! In anything whatsoever! I've never studied computers! Look at all these books here! Shouldn't I at least read classical philosophy? I need some grounding!!" he would lament.

I laughed and said, "I've read all this classical philosophy. And a lot of stuff about organizational theory, macroeconomics, evolutionary theory, formal logic and what have you. And believe me, I would feel completely lost in any of the situations you are describing to me."

Time and again I tried to link his sense of rottenness, lack of substance, and fraudulence to his upbringing. I compared Ben's life style to his father's frugality. I tried to point out to him how difficult it was for him to accept that at age 27 he was making several times the amount of money that his father was making at the end of a distinguished academic career. I tried to get him to connect to the sense of rottenness he had probably felt when comparing his flamboyant sex life with his parents' monogamous devotion to each other. In brief, I tried everything a decent shrink is supposed to do in order to feel that he has earned his monthly check.

I never got so much as an acknowledgment of the usefulness of my ideas. Mind you, this omission would have been easy to accept if Ben had been stupid. But he was brilliant. He just did not seem to care. He had no curiosity whatsoever about the workings of his mind. What mattered to him were the asides I threw in–little pieces of wisdom of Life 101, observations about the difference between his generation and his parents', repeated discussions of how it could be that he was good at something no one could define.

Most of all, the tone of our conversations had changed. I had come genuinely to like Ben, even though there was almost not a single session in which I did not feel exasperated. Only now, instead of "processing my countertransference," I told him that he was straining my nerves or that his jumpiness was driving me crazy. "Sorry, Doctor, that's the client you have," was usually the answer, but he also became more considerate.

Then came a point when his company was setting up a joint venture with a Silicon Valley high-tech firm that possessed exactly the technology needed for the last idea Ben had come up with. His girlfriend was willing to move with him. We discussed the pros and cons for a couple of sessions. Our main conclusion was that it would do him some good to be out of the Tel Aviv party scene and spend half a year in the Bay area, where his girlfriend would paint and he would work hard to integrate his crazy ideas with the technology of their new partners.

During the last session before he left for California, he told me, "It's weird, but I'll miss you. Here I am, having fought with you for one and a half years, driving you crazy, and telling you that none of this is of any help; and now I'll miss you. Life's like a video clip run backwards: it doesn't make any sense."

Mentoring Psychic Growth of Generation Xers

Ben's treatment was, in its own way, helpful. He left it less anxious and confused and with more belief in himself than he had entered it. It turns out that his relationship with his girlfriend has remained stable. He came to appreciate her more deeply and felt fewer qualms about renouncing the pleasures of casual sex.

After about a year Ben came back to Tel Aviv, and founded his own start up company. Once in a while he would come in for a session when things were getting out of hand. He continues to be very successful and to come up with new ideas every few months. He still has no academic foundation, but it seems to me that nowadays he is more comfortable with being who he is.

I have since been in contact with Ben once in a while. He would seek my advice for handling complex human situations in his new startup company. When I saw him function in his work environment, I came to know an aspect of his personality that I had only had glimpses of during the treatment. Ben was warm and supportive towards his employees. I had a chance to talk to several of them, and they all perceived him as tremendously competent and creative, but also fair and emotionally nurturing. It seems that Ben has developed distinct paternal qualities that enable him to be both a role model and a mentor for his employees.

Certainly Ben is not the embodiment of serenity, and he probably will never be. He will probably remain a party animal and enjoy his celebrity status for a long time to come. Part of what makes him successful in his business is that he is, by nature, restless, that his mind and body need constant movement (which made spending time with him in the consulting room, where you are supposed to sit still, a daunting task).

From a more orthodox psychoanalytic point of view his treatment was, to say the least, incomplete. Even though he "got" my interpretations that connected his family history with his sense of emptiness and lack of foundation, the insights did not really matter to him. My attempts at elucidating the transference did not have any impact either.

I believe that what made the treatment useful for him was that, after a long period of time when we had trouble with each other, we found ways to relate to each other meaningfully. Possibly the crucial point was that he received recognition of the value of his talents from "Herr Doktor" (who, incidentally, does not have the faintest understanding of what Ben produces).

Freud (1915) would have called this a transference cure. This treatment might even be characterized as a case of a corrective emotional experience–the nightmare of classical psychoanalysis.

None of my work with Ben had any of the richly layered, multifaceted, meditative quality that characterizes more strictly analytic work (including my own). Ben and I never achieved the atmosphere of timelessness in which past and present become metaphorical embodiments of each other, in which meanings coalesce, crystallize, fall apart, and transform themselves. Neither did we do much work on the transferential enactments in the treatment.

If I had to put the character of my work with Ben in the simplest of terms, I would say that Ben saw in me everything that he was not: I am an academic, in a profession that has been in existence for a century. Sitting with me in the same room brought out all his rage, fear, insecurity, and need for rebellion that he was never able to express toward his father.

His subtle (and sometimes not-so-subtle) devaluation and his little intrusions into my personal space made it very difficult for me to sit with him in the same room. At some point, I came to dislike him intensely. Moreover, I did not have a clue how to help him.

After the blowup, we began to have a more authentic dialogue. I came to appreciate and like him, and I became emotionally significant for him. I accepted him for what he was, admired his abilities, and celebrated his successes. This acceptance, in turn, helped him to become more accepting of himself and to come to terms with the fact that, even though his abilities and talents had no formal definition in the more classical culture to which both his father and I belonged, they were nevertheless very real.

My understanding of Ben's problems gradually shifted, once the dialogue acquired a warmer, more personal quality. I began to think of Ben as caught in an insoluble conundrum. He had grown up in a family shaped by the values of the founding generation of Israel.

His father was a respected academic whose integrity was acknowledged throughout the country, who was asked to sit on committees touching on the most delicate issues of Israeli society. More than anything, his father stood for a combination of dedication to society and clear political beliefs rooted in a long-term historical view of Jewish history. He also represented a cultural view based on clear distinctions and hierarchies: Beethoven belonged to a different category than the Beatles, Goethe could not be compared with Bob Dylan; house, dance, and techno were no music at all but part of a mind-numbing drug culture.

Ben himself had grown up in the world of MTV: a world ruled by 20-somethings in which marketing and culture were inevitably intertwined. The aesthetics of the video clip had formed the standard of his generation, and he lived in a world where ratings were everything.

In his father's world and terms, Ben, indeed, had no foundation; he had no right to authority, because he had neither the formal credentials nor the cultural differentiation that defined legitimate authority. The culture his father represented does not even have names for the new professions.

In the world of Nobrow, Ben is a star. His talents are very real. When he said his activities did not even have a name, he pointed to an objective cultural reality; the culture of information technology is generating roles, activities, and professions that never existed before. His lack of inhibition in combining disparate aesthetic and cultural elements into new structures (which constitutes original sin in the canonic conception of culture) was at the heart of his creativity.

For Ben I represented the traditional cultural heritage of his father. My explicit legitimating of who he was and of his abilities calmed his obsessive doubts that he was a fraud, a worthless impostor, and that nothing about him was real and valuable. In terms of the cultural categories of his parents' generation, he had, as he said, no basis.

Ben loved and respected his father. Yet he could never gain his father's recognition of his talents and achievement. To the extent that I could gain an understanding of the dynamics between them, I got the feeling that Ben's father loved his son from afar. Ben's personality, the world within which he lived, and the work he did were completely foreign to Ben's father. He never voiced any overt disapproval or disdain for his son and the cultural world he lived in, but he seemed to feel remote and possibly intimidated by that world.

Ben had to forgo not only paternal guidance (this, I believe, he managed well), but also paternal recognition. His unrequited yearning for paternal recognition colored his self-experience deeply. In addition, his father's remoteness had deprived him of the possibility of direct confrontation. His frustration and anger at his father's lack of responsiveness never found any direct expression. Ben felt his father's helplessness and bewilderment, and, to protect his father and maintain his idealization of him, he avoided confrontation and relinquished emotional contact.

In the therapeutic relationship, Ben could, first of all, express the rage, disappointment, and anger at his father's generation (to which I did not belong in age, but to which I did belong culturally). By attacking and denigrating me continually, he could express much of the pain that he had accumulated in the years of noncommunication with his father. Ben finally received what he had been yearning for: emotional investment and recognition by a paternal figure. Ben, in his own aggressive way, managed to get me involved. After putting me off balance, he finally received the paternal recognition and emotional contact he had been yearning for.

BETWEEN CANONIC CULTURE AND NOBROW

Some theorists have argued that the pathologies of the late 80s and 90s reflect deep developmental disturbances. First among these theorists is Chasseguet-Smirgel (1984), who sees postmodern culture, with its eradication of differences, as pathological. For her, there is a clear-cut difference between actual aesthetic value as defined by a classical canon and pseudoart, which is based on no real criteria of quality. The lack of differentiation between the truly valuable and the shallow (in Chasseguet-Smirgel's view) pop culture is an indication of the denial between the generation and the sexes and thus essentially perverse.

Similarly, Kristeva (1993) sees postmodern culture as psychically impoverished and impoverishing. She argues that it lacks the capability for deep narration that provides people with the means to symbolize their psychic experience. She agrees with Chasseguet-Smirgel that typical psychopathology is perverse rather than neurotic.

I would like to offer an alternative hypothesis that is kindred to the position of some contemporary authors (Mitchell 1993; Chodorow 1994). The point is not that psychoanalysis widened its scope or that "deeper" pathologies have become more frequent. Psychic structure is in many ways a function of social structure. Freud's writings abound with references to social class. He assumed that neurosis was often the price paid for the demands imposed on those who wanted to belong to the middle classes. In one of his more surprising parables he argued that the daughter of a good family is likely to develop a neurosis along with the chastity imposed on her, whereas a servant girl will stay healthy, albeit losing both her chastity and virginity. (It is not quite clear whose fate Freud considered preferable.)

Post-World War II generations grew up in circumstances very different from Freud's. The Baby Boomers created the social climate of the 60s and 70s. They fought the established social and cultural hierarchies and began to create the much more fluid mode of thinking and living that made issues of identity and self-esteem more critical than conflict around sexuality and aggression.

As the late Stephen Mitchell (1993 ch 1) argued, the needs of Baby Boomers were different from those of earlier generations. Baby Boomers suffered not primarily from repression, but from a difficulty in fully living their subjectivity. Their conception of authority was different from that of previous generations, and, inevitably, so were their needs and desires. Their post-60s conception of authority did not allow for analysts who bring established knowledge of human nature and a position of neutrality into the analytic interaction. Furthermore, analysts like Mitchell (1993 ch 2), themselves Baby Boomers, were not willing to take such a position of unassailable authority and knowledge.

Mitchell was one of the first to argue explicitly against the view that patients could simply be located on a neatly ordered developmental scheme of pathologies. Instead, he understood that psychoanalysis is not a discipline that provides timeless knowledge of human nature but, rather, reacts to a changing human reality of Western societies.

Generation X and Generation Y grew up in a social and psychic reality very different from even that of the Baby

Boomers. Peer-group influence and images from the media are powerful influences on their development. The nuclear families they grew up in are invested with less authority. Their passage into adulthood coincides with the genesis of a culture that was of their own making.

The structure of their psyche is, inevitably, different from structures that evolved in earlier generations of the 20th century. Unlike Freud's generation, they do not think and feel in hierarchic terms. The Baby Boomers rebelled against hierarchies. During the 60s and 70s, a generation of adolescents and young adults attacked the categories that had characterized their parents' world. They fought for sexual freedom; they attacked the right of universities to form curricula on the basis of canonical culture.

Their rebellion is reflected in the writings of theorists who articulated the ideology of the 60s revolution. Philosophers like Foucault and Derrida kept attacking the most basic beliefs of Western culture, from logocentrism to the belief in suprahistorical reason. But they, as well as fellow deconstructionists from Deleuze to Feyerabend, were steeped in the culture they rebelled against. Reading Derrida and Deleuze gives the distinct impression of writers who deconstruct texts that they deeply loved. They tried to show that enlightenment ideals were based on illusory assumptions. But they revered the great enlightenment thinkers from Locke to Kant, whom they deconstructed.

Hence, whether in highbrow or in popular culture, in social liberation movements as well as academic discussion, there was continuity with the canon of the West. As in the struggle of adolescence and postadolescence for individuation, the fight against the earlier generation is carried out against the background of a deep attachment to the current generation. Baby Boomers had emotional contact with the target of their attacks; the authorities they were dismantling had a strong reality for them.

Generations X and Y live in a different world. They have grown into a freedom they did not have to fight for. Unlike the Baby-Boom generation, they do not define themselves as rebels. For many of them, the Western canon is something they may know of but that has very little emotional reality for them: they neither accept nor fight it. The world of Nobrow is precisely defined by its nonrelationship to the Western canon. It is not iconoclastic, because there are no idols, ideals, or works that need to be attacked.

The 60s and 70s, when Baby Boomers came of age, were still characterized by great ideological discussions. Grand intellectual questions still commanded interest for adolescents and young adults. The lectures of Theodor W. Adorno, one of the leading theorists of the Frankfurt school, still attracted huge audiences at the Goethe University of Frankfurt. Michel Foucault's lectures at the College de France and at Berkeley University were grand events, and people fought for seats to attend them.

Generations X and Y grew up in the postideological Reagan-Thatcher era. The struggle of ideologies was a thing of the past. Daniel Bell's (1966) thesis that the end of ideologies had come became a lived reality. Grand intellectual questions seemed to be of little interest; pragmatic considerations were more prominent for GenXers. Therefore, Generation X did not attack previous generations for their authoritarianism, but, rather, for their unquestioned assumption that older generations could expect to be financed by the young (Thau and Hefflin 1997). While Baby Boomers still viewed drug use as a political act of emancipation, GenXers considered it as a way of having a great weekend.

It is easy simply to disqualify Generation X as egocentric, devoid of values, or squeamish and whiny–all these things have been said about them (see Holtz 1995; Thau and Hefflin 1997). Nothing of what I am writing is meant to add to this condemnatory choir. The social and cultural developments I described at the beginning of this chapter were driven by strong historical and technological forces. Generation X could not choose its cultural environment any more than earlier generations could. GenXers have grown into an environment in which the Western canon is not even something worth fighting against, and that environment is not of their making.

ON FORMING AN IDENTITY IN NOBROW CULTURE

Erik Erikson invested a life's work in elucidating the processes of identity formation. In his view there are distinct developmental stages that human beings in all societies go through. Identity formation is the process that begins with adolescents' differentiation from their families. As opposed to children, who define their identity primarily through belonging to a particular family, adolescents begin to seek a sense of who they are that is independent from, and often opposed to, the family's identity and values.

After the stage of adolescent rebellion, the process of identity formation moves further. Identity is beginning to be defined by finding a place in the wider fabric of society. This process involves the acquisition of a role in the workplace and what Erikson (1950) called a sense of generativity. Generativity for Erikson involved both the sense of having something to give and the ability to create a family.

Erikson's (1950, 1968) descriptions were certainly highly adequate to the period in which he wrote. America of the 1950s was a society that was structured mostly around very clearly defined values and social roles. It was, for example, a central fixture of the life expectations of young Americans to establish families.

In the world of Nobrow, the very infrastructure of social roles and hierarchies that defines Eriksonian processes of identity formation has changed dramatically. The cultural changes that I have described make it very unclear how young adults can move into social roles that they know from their parents' generation.

Alexander Mitscherlich's (1967) prediction that Western society was moving in the direction of becoming a fatherless society has become strangely true. The enormous difficulty GenXers have in using their parents as role models has been amply documented (Ellis 1991; Holtz 1995). Fatherlessness is not simply an issue of the failings of individual fathers to provide role models for their children. It reaches much deeper; the very role of fatherhood is cast into doubt.

There are strong indications that in the large cities of the West young adults are not sure at all that they will ever want to found a family. Being single is becoming a viable life style option. Many GenXers seem not to feel the desire or value of raising the next generation. I wonder if, on a deeper level, this reluctance is connected to their sense of detachment from the past. If there is no tradition that is to be handed down and no cultural continuity with the past, why raise a new generation? Many of the more gifted GenXers feel that they do not belong primarily to any particular ethnic, cultural, or national entity. They feel part of the amorphous population of the global village. Their estrangement from previous generations and Western culture is partially a function of this detachment. No cultural tradition or work is canonic; what matters is what can be marketed.

Consequently, their parents feel out of their depth. Many of them feel that their cultural heritage is becoming irrelevant for their children. Some of them fight to pass it on. But others feel that in doing so they become pathetic impediments to their children, and they simply give up on the possibility of truly assuming parental authority (Omer 1999).

Ben's history provides an interesting illustration of this process. His father is a man of remarkable achievement and personal integrity and exemplifies the values that carried the state of Israel through its phase of consolidation. He is devoted as a parent and tried to provide his children with emotional, material, and educational sustenance. Yet he felt completely out of his depth when faced with certain aspects of his son's mental makeup. Being a tolerant and liberal man, he did not want to impose his values and life style on his son. But, as he was not able to understand his son's world, he seems to have become emotionally more withdrawn.

I have come to view Ben's statement that he did not feel he had the right to be angry at his father as sincere. Ben knew that his father had not withdrawn emotionally out of a lack of interest, love, or commitment to his role as father, but out of genuine despair at being able to fulfill his role constructively without imposing something that was foreign to his son's mental makeup and cultural universe. A well-publicized example central to Israeli culture of the 1990s makes this hypothesis more plausible. The Israeli artist who represented most clearly Generation Xers' disenchantment with the Zionist ethos of the previous generation is Aviv Geffen. During the 90s Geffen, who is heterosexual and during the heyday of his career had a long-term relationship with a girlfriend, used to appear with makeup that had a distinctly gender-crossing effect, thus showing his disdain for the Israeli image of masculinity. He had also refused to serve in the IDF. In one of his most famous songs he would scream time and again, "*We are a fucked generation.*" The precise meaning of the Hebrew term *mezuyan* is a combination of two semantic connotations: the first is "having been fucked" in the sense of having been harmed and taken for a ride; the second is being worthless and harmed, that is, fucked up.

Aviv Geffen's concerts would draw huge audiences who knew the lyrics of his songs by heart. And whenever he returned to his song's punchline, "*We are a fucked generation,*" they would scream with him this angry combination of accusation of their parents' generation and despair at their own confusion.

Aviv Geffen's father, Jonathan Geffen, is a well-known writer, playwright, and journalist who has a close relationship with his son and has supported him throughout his career. And Aviv himself has steered clear of the trappings of the career of a rock star. Outside his concerts he was relatively reclusive, tried to avoid excessive attention, and always differentiated between his persona and his right to a quiet private life.

Yet the despair he expressed was, so it seems, genuinely felt and reflected his generation's general feeling. The essence of this despair seems to be that Generation X truly felt that they had no tradition to rely on. The fatherlessness of Generation X was less a matter of individual paternal failures than of a much deeper, cultural process.

Fatherhood, as Lacan (1977) emphasized, is much more than a biological function. It is also the signifier of the cultural order. Lacan's writings abound with references to classical Western culture from Plato to Freud. His underlying assumption was that there is, indeed, a cultural nexus that Westerners are born into and that this nexus reverberates in the unconscious of every member of this culture, whether they know it or not.

The question is whether or not this sentiment holds true nowadays. Is the Western canon from *Antigone* and Aristotle's *Nichomachean Ethics* indeed a part of the philosophy of Generation X? The hypothesis that I am putting forward is that we seem to be witnessing a partial disintegration of this cultural order. The symbolic order that Lacan believed to be constitutive of human existence may be undergoing changes so drastic as to become qualitatively different.

These changes mean that Generation Xers need to form their identities with far less guidance from earlier generations and with less reliance on cultural continuity than did earlier generations. Even the emotional closeness that is created by the act of rebellion is denied to them. They cannot hate their parents for imposing authority on them, and they cannot differentiate themselves through the rebellion that characterized the Baby Boomers. Their acquisition of identity involves the creation of modes of life that are not defined as roles and social functions that previously did not exist.

When Ben complained that he had no basis, he may have been expressing more than an individual predicament. What is easily interpreted as individual psychopathology may be the reflection of a cultural and social upheaval that Fukuyama (1999), for good reason, has called "the Great Disruption." The process of evolving a sense of self seems to be much more experimental and open ended than it was even in previous generations. Ben's qualms in acquiring a stable sense of self exemplify the difficulty of identity formation for Generation Xers.

Chapter 3

The Bobo Dilemma

Yaron: "Maybe I Have No Self-Confidence"

Yaron was tall, powerfully built, fluent, intelligent, reflective, connected to his feelings, and yet he had the right amount of self-irony. He made contact easily and was very open, a pleasure to listen to. In his early 30s, he was currently holding a job in the marketing department of a company that was quickly becoming a major player in one of the emerging technology sectors. He had been in a stable, nurturing, and satisfying marriage for the past two years.

Nevertheless, everything seemed somehow wrong. He hated his job, partially because he found it limiting and boring, partially because it connected to an issue that kept haunting him. The key to our first encounter was, "I'm afraid that the therapy will show that I have no self-confidence whatsoever."

He told me more of his history. His father had been a high-ranking officer in one of Israel's elite ground troops. He had then turned to business, where he was moderately successful for a while but hit a ceiling. Yaron's parents were comfortably off financially, but they suffered because many of his father's peers had become part of Israel's business elite. Nothing was explicitly said about that, but it permeated the family atmosphere.

Overtly the family kept celebrating itself. Owing to the father's army connections, they were still part of Israeli high society. Name dropping was inherent to the family culture, and so was the family lore that they were interesting people. Both parents read a lot and favored intellectual topics of social and political relevance for conversation. The three sons were expected to live up to their parents' standards and were supposed to have interesting opinions on every matter of importance.

Yaron was their third and youngest son. He remembered being an active, physically strong, but overly sensitive child who would burst out crying at insults. Even though no one in the family made fun of him, he felt their silent disapproval.

He was physically very courageous. Always the first to climb a tree, to rappel down the steepest rocks, and to dive from the highest board, he should have felt comfortable with his masculinity, yet he did not. During his adolescence he did not dare approach the girls that he really fancied. His fear of rejection was too great. Even though well accepted by his peers, seemingly cool, and with a good dose of adventurousness, he had the nagging doubt that he was really a wimp. He had begun having sex later than others, and he had had fewer conquests than his peers (or at least fewer than they claimed to have).

When he entered compulsory military service, it was clear to him (and to everybody else) that he would join one of the prestigious commando units that have an almost mythical aura in Israeli society. Those units put enormous demands on their soldiers in every respect: moral, mental, and physical, and they require total dedication to the unit. Basic training lasts 18 months, during which time the soldiers are turned into fighting machines.

Yaron passed the first year of training with flying colors. He had already been short-listed for the next step; there was no doubt that he was to become an officer in the unit. His strength, dedication, openness, courage, and intelligence were beyond doubt.

And then the incredible happened: he showed up before the commanding officer and announced that he was quitting the unit. No one could believe it. They gave him time to think things over. They thought it was a passing whim. But he stuck to his decision.

He demanded to be transferred to an ordinary fighting unit. His official argument was that he could not identify with the unit's ethos of total elitism and had moral qualms about some of the tasks it performed. No one thought for a minute that his quitting was a failure of nerve. The paratrooper unit he transferred to was involved in fighting that was no less dangerous, just more conventional and less secret in its operations.

He completed his army service honorably and started civilian life. For a while he made money using his physical skills and adventurousness. Together with some friends he organized adventure tours in the desert that involved tricky Jeep trails, rock climbing at dangerous sites, and the like. At the time, such tours had just began to become popular, and they made good money.

Then he went to university and, to everybody's surprise, pursued a degree in social work. No one understood his choice: adventurous, powerful, witty Yaron and *social work?* After completing his studies, he briefly worked in the field but then branched out again. He went back to guiding adventure trips, and at the same time went for another first degree, this time in philosophy. He was enthusiastic about logic and the philosophy of language and was encouraged to continue after he earned his B.A.–but he quit.

He decided it was time to start making money. The high-tech sector in Israel was moving into its boom, and it seemed to be the place to go. People tried to prod him into joining a startup company, but he went for a management position in a company that was already well established.

It was at this time that he came to see me. Not only did he hate his job, he had no idea what he wanted to do. Some of his friends had already made a pile of money. He was behind everyone else.

But more than anything he was wondering if he was not a total fake. He had always been considered special. He was the guy who made outlandish choices, who dared to take the less trodden path, who was not influenced by the fashions around him. Adventurous and courageous, he nevertheless opted not to go for the most prestigious army service for moral reasons. Full of initiative and very smart, he decided on social work, because that is what he believed in. He studied philosophy at an age when others were already collecting fat paychecks or had founded their own companies. He was a true individualist.

Yet he was tortured by the idea that all this might be nothing but a myth, a hoax that he had managed to sell both to himself and to his relatives and peers. Maybe he was just a coward. Maybe he would never match his father's distinguished army career. Maybe his choice of social work and philosophy was just a way to perpetuate the myth that he was special, refusing to join the capitalist, macho rat race. Maybe his image of the sensitive intellectual was nothing but a coverup for something very simple: the fear of failure. He harbored the suspicion that behind all his unconventional choices lurked a banal and shameful secret—he lacked self-confidence.

The Therapeutic Dialogue

The therapeutic dialogue gradually moved into the confusing territory of Yaron's experiences as a child and adolescent. His parents, on every measurable dimension, had been dedicated and supportive. They helped where help was needed; they allowed freedom when they thought it advisable. They were typical members of the Ashkenazi elite that had founded and run Israel during the first decades of its existence. They adhered to the honor code of patriotic dedication and of intellectually alert social and political interest and involvement—and everybody was doing very well all the time. Theirs was a generation that did not know the luxury of introspection. Their emotional vocabulary was impoverished, and emotions were legitimate only during times of "objective" duress: if your son was at the war front, if friends had lost a child, if the country was in danger, emotions were legitimate. Otherwise, to speak about one's feelings was a sign of excessive egocentricity or sissiness.

Probably the most important aspect of the therapeutic work Yaron and I did together is best summarized by what the intersubjectivist school (Stolorow, Brandchaft, and Atwood 1987) calls affective crystallization. Yaron gradually acquired a vocabulary that made sense of his contradictory self experience.

Yaron had felt throughout his childhood and adolescence that there were whole areas of his subjective experience that were "excommunicated" from the discourse in his family and the culture they identified with. Yet, because of this excommunication, Yaron could not account to himself exactly *what* was excommunicated.

The result was complex. On one hand, he rebelled against a mode of life that he experienced as impoverishing. Hence his choices went against the grain of what was deemed acceptable in his environment. In particular he rebelled against a conception of masculinity that he experienced as unbearably limiting. On the other hand, the only vocabulary that he had at his disposal to justify his rebellion was a vocabulary of objective values and norms: hence he had to justify in moral terms his dropping out of the elite unit and his choice of academic subjects.

Such justification, indeed, did not correspond to his subjective truth, which, at the time, he could not formulate. His choices were really guided by the feeling that he could not live an authentic life within the confines of the values of his environment. Because he had no vocabulary to formulate this inner truth, he needed to justify his choices within a moral terminology accessible to him and accepted by his environment.

The result was, almost inevitably, that he experienced himself as a cheat. The narrow conception of masculinity that he had grown into led him to distrust his own choices. He was afraid that the true motivation for the life course he had taken was that he was not enough of a man. He simply could not find the words to reconceptualize his meandering course of life as the search for an authentic personal voice.

Time and again, Yaron fell into self-doubt. Should he not go into business? Was he again avoiding the competition that defined a real man? Yet gradually Yaron decided that his overriding desire was to find his personal voice. As we went along, Yaron began to feel more comfortable with himself. He quit the job he hated so much. His open and warm relationship with his wife allowed him to share with her much of the process he was going through. Along with the therapeutic work, he tried out several lines of activity, mostly geared to social involvement in Israel's intractable social and political reality.

In between the various projects he got involved in, he took great pleasure in staying home, reading books, meeting friends for lunch, and going to the beach. He took even greater pleasure in the answer he gave at social occasions when asked what he was doing: "Nothing," he would say with the tremendous sense of relief that comes with ceasing to maintain the typical Bobo persona that would tell how passionate he is about his work.

Yaron's unbearable self-doubts began to abate. He gradually came to believe that people enjoyed spending time with him even though he had no impressive business card to show. He decided to end therapy once he felt he had found a more stable sense of identity and even looked forward to a future that was full of uncertainty.

THE BOURGEOIS BOHEMIANS (BOBOS)

The particular cultural configuration I am investigating through Yaron's story has been exposed and analyzed beautifully by Brooks (2000). Brooks's main thesis has the brilliant simplicity of insights that capture a truth that is right under our noses. He claims that the last decade of the 20th century created a new ethos that merged (or tried to merge) two seemingly irreconcilable sets of values: that of the work- and-money-oriented bourgeoisie and that of the Bohemian search for the authentic life and spiritual self-fulfillment. His term for the new class is, as mentioned in chapter 2, Bobo, a merging of *Bo*urgeois *Bo*hemian.

Brooks (who freely admits that he is a typical Bobo) provides a tongue-in-cheek description of Bobos. He exposes the ironies of the new ethos that seems to square the circle. Nevertheless, he finds the Bobo ethos sympatico.

From a psychotherapeutic point of view, the Bourgeois Bohemian culture is an interesting way of dealing with a quandary that has preoccupied psychodynamic thinking in its various versions: Jungians have dealt with it as the tension between persona and self; Lacan (1977) spoke of it in his investigation of the relation between the subject's desire and alienating identifications; Winnicott (1960) conceptualized it in his writings about the true and the false self; existentialist writings speak of authentic versus inauthentic existence.

As Winnicott (1960) said, the theme of the true and the false self is age old: it has been taken up by almost every religion. The sense that there are ways of living that are more or less authentic, true to our real core, is part of a wide variety of cultures. It has been played out in all kinds of ways—external success versus spiritual existence, true love versus marriage of convenience, vocation versus money—and in the 19th-century Romantic narrative that still hovers over us, adherence to bourgeois values versus the artist's creative self-expression.

Do Bobos, as Brooks's (2000) title, *Bobos in Paradise,* implies (certainly with some irony), really live in paradise? Did the 1990s indeed manage to reconcile money and soul, the search for social status and self-realization? Brooks does not seriously think so. He views the plight of the Bobos with mild irony.

While certainly a well-meaning ideology (who would have anything to say against a form of life that presents you with the best of possible worlds?), it is my clinical impression that Boboism has also created new problems (as if, indeed, the sum total of human unhappiness will always stay constant). Bobo ethics make the harmonious combination of financial success and self-actualization *normative.* Consequently, expectations of life are very high—and the sense of failure when the goal is not reached increases.

My clinical experience of recent years indicates that Brooks's analysis touches on a powerful point. Patients who are in their mid-30s are often torn between the two poles of Bobo ethics. Of course, psychoanalytic investigation can never be content to reduce a patient's conflicts to the current social situation. The particular individual's life course, its complexities, conflicts, pains, and dilemmas, is always a mix of wider social reality and a deeply personal fate.

Years of work with Bobos have led me to conclude that at the heart of their dilemma lies a paradox that is difficult to negotiate. While they are supposed to be guided by their inner need for self-realization, many of them are deeply confused. They feel that everything about them, including their innermost feelings about themselves, is guided by the imperative of success without sacrifice of personal meaning.

Some of them, it seems to me, suffer greatly from this paradox: they feel that the demands put on them to turn everything, from their spirituality to their relationships and their careers, into an effortless work of art creates the opposite of what Bobos are supposed to be—truly free human beings. Hard work needs to be fused with political correctness, financial success with ecological concern, harassing schedules with quality time spent with their children.

THE NEW ETHOS: THE BOURGEOIS BOHEMIANS

The 19th century saw the emergence of the middle classes as the dominant social force in the Western world. An ever-increasing number of people derived their status, wealth, and political power not from noble birth or inherited wealth, but from the fruits of their professional labors (Gay 1989).

The middle class of the 19th century was thin compared with that of the 20th century. It was also much more clearly defined vis-à-vis the "lower classes." The many shadings of middle class that we are used to now did not yet exist. To belong to the middle class, one was expected to live in a house or a large apartment with many rooms. The typical middle-class family had at least four servants and was expected to take long summer vacations at resorts deemed fashionable by the new class.

The new middle class was largely meritocratic: you were expected to build your status on the fruits of the work of the, usually male, head of the family. Diligence, intelligent management of assets, and the display of respectability were the conditions that enabled families to achieve the desired goals. The work-oriented bourgeoisie knew that order, thrift, and hard work are the guide to success. The fall from the middle class could be extremely painful. Social exclusion was swift, and the demands on anything from life style to financial resources were remarkable (Grosskurth 1986).

Many commentators (e.g., Gellner 1985) have argued that Freud's structural model of the personality reflected the concerns of the middle class: the ego was supposed to keep the reigns on all the instinctual demands that could ruin a middle class family. Women, in particular, whose respectability depended on maintaining their chastity and not displaying their sexuality in any overt fashion, had to pay a heavy price for the repressions these strictures entailed (Appignanensi and Forrester 1992).

The cultural countermovement was epitomized in members of the Bohemian class, which exerted a dark fascination on the bourgeois mind (Seigel 1986). Bohemians were both feared and envied. Bohemian women were a source of attraction, and dark forces could destroy good boys by drawing them into the quagmire of bottomless sensuality. Bohemian culture was ambivalent toward the Bourgeoisie: in part it ridiculed the stifling and limited way of life, yet many Bohemians were themselves bourgeois who had lost social status because of financial problems (Seigel 1986 ch 4).

The 20th century continued to highlight the contrast between bourgeoisie and Bohemia in many variations. To mention only two recent manifestations, we have the hippie culture of the 1960s and the Yuppie culture of the 1980s.

The 1960s brought about a movement that attacked capitalist, bourgeois values in an all-out indictment. It pervaded popular culture–its mode of life, its music, its lyrics, and its sexual mores. Intellectuals like Herbert Marcuse and Norman O. Brown pitted the erotization of life against the heartless, mechanical life form that emptied people of their vitality and libido (Roszak 1969).

Social commentators are sharply divided in their assessment of the social revolution brought about by the 1960s and 1970s. Some see it as the great liberation from the stifling sexual repression of the 50s and as a great mind-opening movement (Roszak 1969; Paglia 1989). Others see it as the great catastrophe that ruined the moral fabric and the cultural heritage of Western culture (Frum 1999; Kimball 2000).

Whatever one's position on the 1960s revolution may be, the 1980s brought a strong conservative backswing. Primarily they rehabilitated one of the main bourgeois themes: making money was good, and the more you made, the better. Neoconservatives combined an emphasis on family values with deregulation of the financial markets. Deregulation, in turn, allowed for previously unheard of financial success stories. Ever-more daring corporate raiders created a boom of mergers and acquisitions that, in turn, created a bonanza for newly popular investment bankers. What had been a pin-striped, conservative world with strict codes now turned into an exciting world of takeover battles. The new freedom of capital flow allowed people in their 20s to make their first millions just because they had the knack of buying and selling bonds and stocks in the right split second.

The new category of the Yuppie was born. Depicted mercilessly by Tom Wolfe (1986) in *The Bonfire of the Vanities,* this class did not see greed and unbridled jockeying for position and success as a vice. These were, indeed, the ultimate virtue. Sixtyish downdressing gave way to the great wave of status symbols: Armani suits, Rolexes, Mercedeses, and reservations at the most expensive restaurants were now what it took to be somebody.

After the brief recession at the beginning of the 1990s, two momentous changes occurred: an unprecedented, technology-driven economic boom coincided with a power shift from conservatives to liberals like Blair and Clinton. If the investment banker had been the symbol of financial success in the 1980s, the high-tech entrepreneurs of Silicon valley dominated the headlines in the 1990s. Concurrently new media created jobs that had not even existed. If greed and financial acumen were the great virtues of the 1980s, creativity became the catchword of the 1990s.

It was this constellation that gave birth to the new social category of the Bobos, which Brooks (2000) describes so aptly. Greed was out, personal development was in. Armani suits were out; Timberland and other manufacturers that showed one's connectedness to nature were in. Unbridled ambition was out; the search for expressing one's unique selfhood was in.

But the Bobos did not produce a dropout mentality. The anticapitalist rhetoric of the 1960s had lost its foundation with the crumbling of the Iron Curtain and the end of the Cold War. Capitalism and liberal democracy had won the contest for good (or so it seemed). One of the most perspicuous commentators of the social and political scene claimed that we had arrived at the end of history (Fukuyama 1992).

The point was not to oppose capitalism; the Blair-Clinton liberal way that had been prepared by intellectuals like Giddens (1993) was about to create capitalism with a human face. And the Bobos were the prime representatives of this new capitalism.

There were, of course, some paradoxes involved here: high-tech startups could do with no less than 16-hour workdays on their way to the grand exit that was going to make millions for its founders and employees. The competition demanded frenzied work around the clock.

So where was the human face of the new, global capitalism? The answer was as simple as it was brilliant: none of this hard work was drudgery directed toward only money and status. Your company was the place where your creativity could flourish most fully. Synergetic relationships with your team replenished your spiritual energies; and, since you were realizing your potential, you were in a constant state of flux. You were supposed to work very hard, not because you strove for money and status, but because your work had become your way to self-fulfillment. You were creative in what you did (it did not matter whether you managed a mutual fund, ran a magazine, practiced law, or worked in marketing–you did it creatively) and hence derived a deep spiritual satisfaction from your work.

The circle had finally been squared. Gone was the specter of the company man of the 50s who sold his soul to his job. For the first time in history, you could be a self-realizing, self-expressive, tender-minded, nature-connected romantic who made loads of money. The cruel opposition between bourgeois and Bohemian was gone. The Bobo was born.

The problematic of the Bobo generation was that the demands of life (and hence on the self) had become both very high and, in a sense, paradoxical. The 1980s reinforced financial success as the ultimate touchstone of success and status. But the new elites could no longer afford to be driven by greed and status hunger. To be more precise, the Bobos' life narrative was not about money and power.

They looked down at those who were driven and who exhibited status symbols in the manner of "conspicuous consumption." Even if you had the money, you were not supposed to drive, say, a Jaguar or a Mercedes, because that would mean that you wanted to show off. You could spend the same amount of money, though, on a sports-utility vehicle, because that would show that you were not one of those locked into a conventional life style but, rather, that you had a distinctive taste for adventure.

Bobos were not allowed to be nerds; just to be a hard-working achiever was not "in." They were supposed to have a sense of adventure, they must do something that showed that they transcended the simple command "make money and achieve status." The money and the status were supposed to be byproducts of their creative self-realization.

Brooks (2000) shows how a whole industry caters to the need of Bobos to project an image that was not supposed to be concerned with image. He goes into great detail to describe Bobos' studied casualness, the subtleties of the new codes that showed that they belonged to the new class of those who transcended simple, brutish Yuppies and reached the new heights in the search for spiritual fulfillment.

Cyberspace Mobility and the Tightening of Career

The downside of globalization was not officially integrated into the Bobo ethos. It was the existential panic that the new economy was the kingdom of the young. It was not just that you could leave your mark quickly; you *must* do it in time—and that generally meant by your mid-30s at the latest.

The social structure of today provides most of us with a freedom that was unimaginable in the past. In the Western world there are, in principle, no social boundaries that cannot be crossed. The circumstances of your birth do not preclude your doing anything or becoming anything you wish. Aristocracy by birth is a vanishing class. Except in limited circles, old money has ceased to be more valuable than new money. The nouveau riche have become the self-made people, and, in today's culture, this status is often more admired than that of an heir to the family fortune.

Gender (again, in principle) imposed no limitation on what one could do. Women have been prime ministers of major countries like France and Britain and CEOs of major companies. Sexual orientation may still be a problem, but, at least in Europe and even in the United States, there are openly gay politicians in prominent positions. Of course, we are as yet a far cry from true equality for all, but we seem to be on our way.

Postmodernism has come to mean that no category is seen as fixed anymore. Anything from traditional family structure, parenting, and gender role can legitimately be questioned, and there seems to be a gradual and consistent move toward true liberalization of society. In any cosmopolitan society, mobility is increased because previous acquaintances and connections have become less important than they were well into the 1970s. Society offers well-defined tracks with powerful rules, and being somebody means to "make it" along one of these tracks.

In turn, every individual becomes a commodity that can be marketed almost everywhere. With one condition, though: you need to fit some type of brand category that is internationally recognizable. Not unlike internationally recognized brand names from Mercedes to Giorgio Armani to Rolex, you need to be associated with some category that places you on the level of quality on which you want to be traded.

In principle, there are no limitations on who can be accepted into prestigious MBA programs like Harvard's. But not having a prestigious MBA can easily preclude your embarking on certain career tracks. And career tracks define who you are. Because the village has become global, you no longer need to know the chief of the tribe to get a job. But you do need to fit into some category that will place you in a slot in a social hierarchy that has moved from privilege of birth to privilege of achievement. The self, while less limited by accident of birth, now has become a commodity whose value is determined by the price it fetches on the market.

There is freedom, but there is also incredible pressure. At a very early age, people begin to understand that their CVs, their business cards, or, as Jungian psychology would call it, their *personae,* will determine their fates. Anything from the shape of your abdominal muscles to the level you reached at Merrill Lynch will define who you are and what you can get. This holds true on a variety of dimensions: great looks may open doors of model agencies, brains at high-tech startups or investment banks. Both may turn you into a millionaire at an early age.

It seems as if there are no limits to self-creation: if you work hard enough, you can change from wimp to body builder, from social misfit to the life of the party, from underling to mover and shaker. It also means that, because the global village, by its very existence, has given you all the opportunities, you can blame only yourself if you have not made it. The world belongs to those who have the guts to make the most of their natural talents.

There are clear indications of having made it: the color of your credit card; the make of your watch and of your car; the size, quality, and location of your apartment or home; and your clothes. Even those who spurn those visible status symbols nevertheless have internalized the myriads of codes that define the extent to which they have made it.

There is no escape from these codes. They follow you into your bedroom, even into the most private recesses of your mind. Career success is not enough; you must have a lot of fun, too, including enough sexual adventure and a variety of sexual tastes.

During the Internet craze of the 1990s, Israel came to have the highest density of high-tech companies per capita in the world, and it looked as if it was about to become the Silicon Valley of the Middle East. (There is a certain irony to my writing this several years after the NASDAQ went into a nosedive, and with it an overwhelming majority of the startups; and there is tragedy, too, in writing this while the dream of peace between Israel and the Palestinians has given way to bloodshed and horror.) The most sexy persona was therefore to be able to say, "I am the CEO of a startup company." Investment banking and venture capital were the next two categories that exuded some sex appeal as they were connected to the craze of the new economy. The only other category that had similar sex appeal was being a hotshot in the media (the 1990s also brought an enormous expansion in the media industries).

Anything else was inferior. Lawyers (except at the highest tier), physicians (except hotshot surgeons), and most of the other established professions exuded an aura of staleness. Those professionals had missed the really sexy high-speed train and were stuck on the old local train.

The incredible mobility made possible by the new economy exerted great pressure on the Bobos' psyche. At parties you can see the young stars of the economy, the entrepreneurs of high-tech (or biotech) startups. Some of them have sold their companies after about three years of excruciating work and are now worth anywhere between 100 million and a billion dollars—and some of them are not yet 30 years old. Those who are not (yet) there watch anxiously: "I'm 32 and, so far, not even close to my exit. Have I fallen behind?"

As everything seems to be possible, you have no one to blame but yourself if you have not made it big. There are too many examples of entrepreneurs whom you have either met personally, read about in the papers or news magazines, or seen on television. If you are stuck somewhere midway on the ladder, it is very difficult to blame the circumstances. Whatever extenuating circumstances you can cite, there is always a successful startup zillionaire whose starting point was worse than yours.

This leads us to the heart of what I would call the Bobos' dilemma. During the heyday of the Yuppie, concern for one's persona was nothing to be ashamed of. The hyperbolic satire of this period, Bret Easton Ellis's (1990) *American Psycho,* ritualistically goes through long descriptions of the brands each of the participants is wearing: attention to the last detail of style was driven to ultimate excess.

Bobos are not supposed to care for their personae in this overtly flamboyant style. Nevertheless, Bobos invest in their personae with at least as much care as did the Yuppies of the 80s (Brooks 2000). But this investment is carefully guarded. There is a whole industry that helps create personae that make it clear that Bobos are beyond caring about their personae. They spend no less money on their clothes than Yuppies did. But the clothes exude a stylish casualness and a concern with comfort, are made of natural materials. and evoke a slight tinge of nostalgia for the simpler ways of life.

The Bobos' predicament is no less complex than the Yuppies', if anything, it is more complex. Financial success remains as important as it was during the 1980s, but Bobos have to be able to achieve it without seeming to care.

YARON AND THE BOBO DILEMMA

How did Yaron negotiate the Bobo dilemma? Some aspects of Yaron's story are well known psychoanalytic themes: the quest to find one's personal voice behind alienating identifications, the intergenerational conflict between the values and life styles of his parents' generation and Generation X, to which Yaron belongs. These themes played crucial roles in the therapeutic dialogue, a dialogue that greatly helped Yaron to attenuate the self-doubt that had tortured him for so many years.

Another aspect of Yaron's predicament, which, even though highly individual in its particular configuration, reflects tensions and conflicts that are characteristic of his generation in the Western world. Yaron experienced the world as one vast field of opportunity. He was faced with the necessity to choose. His choices were made difficult by three cultural commands. The first, "Be a man and take on the world big time"; the second, "make as much of a success of yourself as possible"; the third,

"Realize your own, personal potential and find your own personal voice."

Given the enormous importance that traditional values and images of masculinity have in Israeli culture, Yaron could not rid himself of the constant suspicion that the choices that seemed to turn him into an individualist were not genuine. A man first and foremost had to be a man; he had to be a hero, a go-getter, and amass as much power and money as possible. If he didn't, it was because he was a wimp. This cultural narrative was his family's heritage, and it was part and parcel of the culture of the army that had played such a great role in his upbringing. Hence he simply could not rid himself of the suspicions that he harbored toward his choices.

I do not, by the way, exclude the possibility that Yaron's quitting the elite unit in the army was partially guided by a feeling that he was not cut out for this type of service. After having worked with several men who successfully completed their service in such units but have remained scarred for the rest of their lives, I have a hunch that, for many of them, Yaron's choice would have preserved their mental integrity. But such was the pressure for heroic masculinity in Israeli culture (it changed in the 1990s) that many of them chose to stay with something their psyche will not be able to metabolize for the rest of their lives.

Hence Yaron's suspicion may have contained a grain of truth. But it was part of our therapeutic work to help him reconceptualize the suspicion that he did not have it in him. He most certainly could have served in the elite unit, but he would probably have sustained irrevocable psychological harm. In that sense, the choice he made may well have been very healthy.

There is yet another aspect of Yaron's dilemma. A large proportion of Bobos buy wholesale into the thesis that authenticity, self-realization, and personal development, on one hand, and financial success and the attainment of social status, on the other, are consistent with each other. Not only that, the hard work they do is supposed to constitute self-realization.

For some this can certainly be true: people who have an overriding talent that harmonizes with their central character traits often have a sense of destiny or calling and truly feel that they realize their personal potential in what they are doing.

This can also be true for business people. I have worked with many people who have natural business talent, who truly enjoy their work and are highly creative in it. But, alas, they are a relatively small minority. For most of us, life entails a delicate balance between our desires for money, status, power, and security and our needs for meaning, personal satisfaction, and emotional richness.

Yaron was ambivalent about the Boboic myth of the ultimate combination of self-realization and professional success. On a conscious level, he bought into it, partially because it was the dominant myth of his age cohort. He believed that risk-taking entrepreneurship was what ultimately brought fulfillment to those who had the talent and the guts to go for the top. Given his constant doubts about his masculinity, he was, of course, prone to interpret his failure to find the ultimate combination of money and fulfillment simply as a failure of courage.

Nevertheless, he was suspicious of the cultural myth of Boboism, even though he had trouble articulating his suspicion. He had grown up in a family that refused to acknowledge any emotion that was not consistent with the dominant cultural paradigm of their time and place. This suspicion had made Yaron sensitive to the type of disavowal that is necessary for many contemporary Bobos to claim that they enjoy their grueling, 16-hour work days.

Yaron's way out of the Bobo dilemma was to go explicitly for one of its horns. He dropped out of the race for money and status and, for a time, chose to give himself a new identity—to do nothing, to find his own voice. He had come to the conclusion that, at least during this period of his life, the Boboic alchemy that fuses hard work with spiritual and personal fulfillment could not work for him.

THE BOBO TRAP: THE NECESSITY FOR A MARKETABLE PERSONA

I believe that Yaron's plight cuts to the heart of the paradox of Boboism. Overtly it is about fusing success and personal fulfillment. But what Bobos hide anxiously from themselves and others is that their culture is far more other directed than its members admit to themselves. While the more traditional bourgeois societies had their anxiously preserved status symbols, against which the new culture defines itself, Bobos have evolved their own codes that define whether or not one has made it.

In fact, their plight is particularly difficult if the tightening of career deadlines is considered. There always is the strong possibility that you will find yourself an outsider at the global party of those who got their entrance tickets in time, that is, by their early 30s.

Yaron's suffering was an amalgam of his doubts about his masculinity and the typical Bobo fear that he had missed his chance to be part of the boom of the 1990s. He did not find his slot in one of the more sexy categories of the new economy and hence did not have a persona that was deemed sexy.

Yaron's dropping out of the race was no less about quitting the panicky search for a sexy Bobo persona than it was about dropping the issue of diamond-hard masculinity. By deciding to quit the race, Yaron was actually embarking on a courageous experiment. He wanted to find out if it was possible to stay alive with no business card at all. Amidst his confusion about what his true desires were, Yaron came to the conclusion that he was not going to feel authentic about anything if he did not finally do something drastic.

FINAL REFLECTIONS: HOW CAN WE SPEAK OF THE GOOD LIFE?

It is tempting to read my rendering of Yaron's story as an indictment of Boboism, as an implicit endorsement of an anticapitalist stance, or even as some kind of post-1960s "drop-out" ideology. I endorse none of these positions. Being a product of my times, I am as prone to the Bobo dilemma as are many of my contemporaries. Despite all the irony with which I have represented the Bobo fusion of Hippie and Yuppie, I find myself faced with the very same conundrum as my cohort: I, too, strive to combine money and personal fulfillment, adventure and safety. I invest as much in my persona as any other Bobo does in his.

I do not look upon the complexities of creating a Bobo persona with either disdain or moral superiority. I do not know of any way of life that does not entail concern for one's persona. Neither do I subscribe to some ideology (New Age, Jungian, or otherwise) that puts inner values (the self, spirituality, the feminine side) above external success. The point of telling Yaron's story is not to glorify his retreat inside, or his dropping out of the race for the business card. Nor am I arguing against concern for one's persona. My intention is to analyze an, albeit unusual, attempt to deal with the complexity of identity formation in the age of the Bobos.

I am not presenting Yaron's story as the recipe for everybody. For Yaron, the retreat from the race served a wide variety of purposes. It needs to be seen within the complexity of his family background. His move cut a Gordian Knot he had been tied up with for most of his life. He opted for a vocabulary that put personal meaning and the development of his subjectivity at the center without trying to embellish it. Yaron could finally simply say, "That's what I want right now," without having to justify it either by the ethos of masculine heroism in which he had grown up or by the Boboic language that merges money and personal growth. He finally acquired a sense of authorship over his life (Strenger 1998)

My conclusions are, of necessity tentative. On the basis of my work with Yaron and several other patients who had similar problems in navigating the complex course of Bobo existence (Strenger 1998, 2003), I am inclined to think that, while the new cultural ideal is in and of itself laudable, it creates intractable problems for many of those who identify with its ideology. Many of them feel that they are living a lie. All the talk of their creativity conceals hard work. In addition, as the media are inundated with the great success stories, those who have made just decent careers for themselves really feel that they have failed, even if, by most standards, they are doing quite nicely.

Bobos are, of course, not a homogenous group. Hence therapeutic work with them will be guided by the particular constellations of their characters, their personal histories, developmental deficits, conflicts and traumas (Strenger 1998). In Yaron's case, we have seen how the particular constellation of his upbringing gave his conflicts and questions their unique character.

Nevertheless in working with Bobos, questions about what constitutes the good life are unavoidable. I have, in many instances, found that fruitful therapeutic interaction with them almost always contains a certain amount of philosophical dialogue (Strenger 1998; see also ch 9). I do not mean instruction in professional philosophy, but common reflections on the presuppositions about what the good life consists of–questions like whether or not the Bobo ideal of life is feasible; whether Love (with a capital "L") is a myth or a reality to be sought after; and about the intricate relationship, and often conflict, between self-realization and commitment to spouse and family.

Such a dialogue seems, on the face of it, closer to philosophical counseling than to psychoanalytic or psychotherapeutic work in the conventional sense. My sense is that we cannot refrain from conducting such dialogues without avoiding the responsibility that Hoffman (1999) has formulated so poignantly: to help the patient, who has a limited amount of time, to live a better life.

Chapter 4

Failing Fathers, Failing Sons

The Idea of Psychoanalytic Mentoring

The last decade has brought significant changes in the conception of analytic work. As Mitchell (1993) argued, psychoanalysis is undergoing a deep paradigm change. The goal of analysis is conceived of less as making the unconscious conscious than as the enrichment of a patient's subjectivity. One of the most eloquent spokesmen of this direction of thought, Bollas (1989, 1992), developed an interesting vocabulary to describe the process of elaborating a patient's personal idiom.

This chapter explores the movement of contemporary psychoanalysis from the deconstructive to the elaborative aspect of the therapeutic process. This movement emphasizes that the analytic process is primarily constructive rather than analytic in the classical sense of the term (i.e., primarily making the unconscious conscious). Hence, my argument is that much of what transpires in the analytic process can be seen as mentoring the patient's growth.

The project of individuality is an attempt to give form to materials that are given by the individual's fate. To live a life is, therefore, analogous to the work of the *bricoleur* (Strenger 1998). Unlike the studio artist, the *bricoleur* does not buy in stores geared to fulfilling an artist's needs. The *bricoleur* roams through junkyards, cellars, and attics to find the materials for his works, which, in turn, take shape through his meeting with the *objets trouvés,* objects found by chance in the junkyard, because he cannot, or will not, use materials designed for the creation of art.

Using the metaphor of self-creation by the *bricoleur* (Strenger 1998) provides an additional perspective on the therapeutic relationship: it is an attempt to help people who have gotten stuck with their search for authorship. They turn to therapy because they feel that they cannot turn their lives into a creation that they identify with. They are *bricoleurs,* who say, "I cannot turn the base materials I was given into a life that I experience as truly mine and as truly worth living."

Facilitating a patient's search for authorship means to help the patient move out of the sense of fatedness and the feeling that it will never be possible to live a life that is truly hers or his. Once we conceptualize the process of analytic therapy as helping the patient to restore a sense of authorship, the question arises, what are the clinical implications of this process? We are talking about an essentially synthetic process, and the metaphor of psycho-'analysis' may not be a good way of describing this process. The analyst's input in this synthetic process is, inevitably, much more substantial than the classical model of neutrality has assumed.

There is a spectrum of views of the place of the analyst's subjectivity. At one end I would place the Kleinians (see Schafer 1997). Even though they write extensively about countertransference, they always interpret it as what the patient puts into the analyst. Similarly Ogden (1995), even though he speaks of an analytic third that is a co-creation of two subjectivities, and even though he provides extensive accounts of his own trains of thought and emotion, ultimately always seems to imply that his subjective processes are somehow influenced by the patient.

At the other end, relational psychoanalysis emphasizes the impact of the analyst's actual subjectivity (see Mitchell and Aron 1999). In the last decade, a growing number of analytic writers have begun to think along similar lines. Irwin Z. Hoffman (1983) was among the first to consider the idea that the analysand's decoding of the analyst's *actual* subjectivity is of great importance. Stephen Mitchell (1993) argued that the analyst's becoming enmeshed in the patient's hopes and fears is a crucial factor in determining therapeutic success. Adam Phillips (1995) has gone further to argue that psychoanalysis is primarily a dialogue that aims to make human beings more interesting to themselves.

While the contemporary literature has made important progress in dismantling the illusion of neutrality and in emphasizing the irreducible importance of the analyst's actual subjectivity, I think that we may not have gone far enough. It is my sense that a great deal of contemporary analytic writing still tries to put more weight on correct technique and sees the analyst's total being as only one, albeit crucial, ingredient in the therapeutic process.

If, indeed, assisting the patient's search for authorship is central to the therapeutic process, the role of mentor may be a more appropriate model for much of what transpires in analytic work. Yet the very notion of mentoring implies a much more direct impact of the analyst's personality, values, and beliefs on the patient than does the original image of the neutral analyzer. We need to go one step further. The existentialist tradition has always argued that the psychotherapeutic relationship involves the totality of the therapist's being, including her deepest values and beliefs. Existentialists from Ludwig Binswanger (1935) through Rollo May (1958) to Irvin Yalom (1980) have argued for decades that we stick to our theories about what makes therapy work, whereas other factors (that we consider little diversions from the "serious" work) may be of greater importance. Existentialism has always assumed that psychotherapy of all sorts is primarily a human relationship that is structured by rules and boundaries.

What if we were to shift the weight around and say that psychoanalysis (like every other form of psychotherapy) is primarily a relationship involving the analyst's whole being? It would mean that what we call technique is primarily a way to impose discipline on this relationship. This discipline is, of course, of the utmost importance, because it makes it possible to put the analyst's personality to *therapeutic* use.

My point might seem semantic, but I think that it entails a reconceptualization of what psychoanalysis is. It is not a technique that involves, among other things, the analyst's subjectivity. It is a relationship in which the analyst's whole psychesomatic being is engaged, a relationship that is governed by socially sanctioned rules that define the therapist's status and responsibility. This is why I prefer the term the analyst's "being" or "personality" to the currently used term subjectivity. The latter term is defined by its semantic relationship to "objectivity" and hence implies that the relationship is *also* influenced by the analyst's subjectivity while allowing a certain amount of objectivity.

Let me now relate my work with a young man whose views about what had made the therapy work forced me to rethink the nature of the analytic relationship and the concept of analytic mentoring.

AMOS: "I'M AN EMPTY SHELL"

The young man (I was tempted to say the boy) in my consulting room looked self-assured, slightly bored. "Everything comes very easy to me. I'm not always sure that I really want to do what I am doing, because I get bored quickly," he said. I got a bit irritated. Amos was tall, athletically built, good looking. His countenance was aloof, his tone slightly arrogant. I was wondering, if everything is so great, why did he come to see me?

Yes, there was a problem. He sometimes thought that he might be homosexual. No, he had never had any homosexual relationships, but somehow his sexual relationship with his girlfriend was not satisfying. He often did not feel like having sex and, when he did, he often felt overwhelmed by his girlfriend's intense passion. So maybe he was homosexual after all.

The first session left me somewhat confused. I generally get a sense of a patient's suffering in the first interview, even though I long ago got rid of the need to come up with brilliant hypotheses about the dynamics and etiology of a patient's problems right away. Here I somehow could not make head or tail of them. I do not think people turn to therapy if they are not genuinely suffering. Something about Amos's aloofness and touch of arrogance made it impossible for me actually to feel what he was like.

In the next session I was surprised to find him very different. He looked much more like a boy now, a frightened boy. Instead of a bored genius, he seemed to be a boy terrified of being on the verge of ruining his life. He was a student of art history and aesthetics. He had won a prize in his first year for an outstanding essay; he had gotten a scholarship in his second year; but since then Amos had flunked pretty much every course he took. The university was on the verge of withdrawing his scholarship, and the professors who had supported him were deeply disappointed. There was one lecturer who still believed in him, but Amos's credit was soon going to be used up.

This time I could feel Amos's genuine need for help. I thought to myself, "My God, if, at the university, he puts on the arrogant façade I saw last time, and if he continues not to meet his course requirements, no wonder they are on the verge of kicking him out." In subsequent sessions, I experienced Amos as being horrified by a world that was far too big for him.

Yes, he had written brilliant papers on the impact of Nietzsche's writings on Rothko's work. Those papers had made some of his professors feel that he might have real genius. But now, when he looked at paintings, all he could see were blotches of color. He could not really *see* the paintings. The wonderful pleasure he had once known when he saw aesthetic structures was a thing of the past. Now he could only feel panic. It was, he said bitterly, the same as he felt with his girlfriend, for whom he lost any desire when she touched him.

"I am really an empty shell" Amos said. "Everything about me is completely fake. Sometimes I feel as if I have no inside at all. I feel dead. I look at a painting, I read a poem, and I don't see anything. It's blah, blah, blah. Red, white, blue. Pure nonsense. Maybe all that stuff I wrote was nothing but bullshit. I somehow managed to impress them. They're calling my bluff. They will drop me like a hot potato. And then I will be nothing."

Sometimes during the first month I mused, what would have happened if I had expressed my irritation at Amos's arrogance in the first session? His façade of nonchalant arrogance was convincing at first. You could easily mistake it for the whole truth about him. I could easily imagine how his arrogance could make people feel that he was a cheat and a liar who just played for time. He kept making promises about seminar papers that he was about to hand in. And then he would sit in the library. The texts in aesthetic theory that had once been his delight did not mean a thing. Sometimes he wondered if he actually knew the language they were written in.

"I can't fuck up. If I bring them a great paper, the type I used to write in my first year, they'll forgive me my lies, all the times I didn't show up for exams. I *must* produce the big time thing. I must. But I can't see. I can't understand!"

Within a month or two Amos came to trust me to the point where he could truly share his panic with me. My irritation had quickly given way to a fatherly worry about this young man who was on the verge of ruining his name at the university. He had been referred to me because of my background in philosophy. And sometimes, haltingly, he would mention a word or two about some book he saw on my bookshelves that he had read. I felt that he did not dare to say what was truly on his mind. He was beginning to believe that I might actually care about his well-being. But what if I found out what a cheat he was? I would dump him like a hot potato.

I had taught in interdisciplinary programs in the history and philosophy of science, and my own writing is seated mostly in between disciplines. When a student begins to talk, I can sense if a movement of thought is right, much as you can see on a tennis court if someone is a "natural." There are people who might be good players, but they simply do not have that flow or timing that comes when they just "have it." And Amos had it, big time. His was a truly first-class mind with an amazing ability to move between conceptual worlds.

My strategy was to get Amos off his project of writing the masterpiece that would convince everybody that he was a true genius. He had come to see me at the beginning of the spring term, and I thought that it would be useful for him simply to try for a while to be an ordinary student who did his homework and passed his tests. During the first months I did not know what his real abilities were, since he was careful not to talk shop. I definitely thought that he was intelligent, but after this brief interlude, it began to dawn on me that Amos's might be a mind of truly extraordinary quality.

My association with naturals in tennis turned out to be apt. When Amos was 11 years old, a trainer had seen him on the tennis court and recognized him as a natural. He was taken into a program at the Israeli Tennis Centre that was designed to foster talented players. He made enormous progress in no time. He quickly grew tall and soon began to develop a first-rate serve-and-volley type of game. When he reached 15, some of his serves were timed at 200 kilometers an hour, and his opponents began to dread his ability to put them under enormous pressure with his approach shots and his uncanny ability to cover the net. The coaches of the national team were seriously considering putting him on the Davis Cup team when he was 16.

Then suddenly he lost it. In particular, he lost the weapon that had made his opponents dread him, his serve. "I would stand on the court, and suddenly I had absolutely no idea how to play a serve. It was as if I had never held a tennis racket in my hand. The worst was my ball throw—it went all over the place but never where I wanted it to be." Double faults began to accumulate, and the national trainers soon dropped the idea of putting him on the national team. He still played tournaments but only on a local level.

Smiling boyishly, Amos said, "Sometimes for a set or so, it comes back. I can feel what it is like when I am myself on the court. The serve movement flows, I go up to the net, and I just *know* where the ball is going to be. And then it disappears again. I expect it to disappear, and then I just wait for it to be over. I mostly lose. But it's fun while it lasts. . . . Sometimes it drives me crazy, though, to feel what kind of tennis player I could have been." And then, for moments, he would go into a helpless rage: "For God's sake. I *know* I have it. But it's as if there is an inner saboteur who won't let me be who I can be. And then I'm back to my empty shell. I'm alive for half an hour, and then it's gone."

Well, I thought, there is a perfect example of self-defeating behavior. A boy with amazing athletic and intellectual abilities who consistently kills off his own attempts to capitalize on his inborn talents. Why is that the case?

When Amos took a test at the university, he would observe himself from the outside. "I feel like a walking corpse. My movements are those of a robot. Once I receive the questions, my mind feels like the inside of one of those extraterrestrial machines in the *Exterminator* movies. I register them, I categorize them, and my mind feels dead." More often than not, he would hand in an empty test form and leave the classroom. Then, sitting outside, he would feel like a burned-out shell and wonder if he had anything like a soul.

Frozen Sexuality

After several months, Amos began, haltingly, to speak of his sexual fantasies. To be more exact, he did not really have sexual fantasies, but, rather, a fetish: he would buy body-building magazines and masturbate to the images of posing body builders. Sometimes the body builders were male, sometimes they were female.

I asked him if there were any plots, any fantasies. No, there were not. He just looked at the images and masturbated mechanically. It would be over in a couple of minutes. He would experience physical orgasmic release, but no real experience of climax. He continued to have very little sex with his girlfriend, with whom he otherwise had a very warm relationship. He loved her, and she adored him. But she constantly felt rejected by him because he would not sleep with her. It turned out that it was not just her passion that was too much for him. It was also her very physicality, which completely closed him off. He smiled apologetically and said, "You must understand, Carlo. She is truly there, a physical, live human being. I'm just an empty shell. I feel *invaded* by her physicality. It's too much for me. I don't have anything to pitch against her sheer physical presence. and then there is nothing left of me. Maybe I'm just gay, and that's it. Because it doesn't really matter for me whether the body builders are male or female."

It seemed to me that Amos's sexuality was completely frozen. I told him, "You know, sexual fantasies are generally like videos. But yours just seem to be stills. There is no movement, and there is no plot. Just an image. And it isn't even an image that stems from your imagination. It's just a photograph from a magazine. Maybe you could try to take one of these images and make it come alive. Construct a plot around it that you find exciting. You know, our sexual fantasies are generally ways of dealing with our deepest pains, but they do so in a very covert form. Maybe if you could gradually unfreeze the stills and turn them into moving pictures, we could get an idea of what is hidden behind those silent images."

"It seems to me," I said, "that your feeling of being an empty shell is reflected in the fact that you do not allow yourself really to have sexual fantasies. It is as if you have had to deep-freeze your sexuality in order *not* to know what is behind your fantasies. Maybe you can risk taking a peek now."

Amos took the homework seriously. He tried to fantasize rather than just sticking to the stills. It was not easy for him;

initially his imagination would simply go blank. But gradually something began to happen. He began to notice that the pictures that excited him the most were those in which two body builders posed near each other. And then, even though there was no fantasy with a plot and movement yet, it suddenly dawned on him that what he saw was like a cartoon in which two men or two women posed with each other, *and the smaller, or younger, one turned out to be stronger than the older and bigger one.* This was the clue that gradually led to the heart of the pain that Amos had frozen inside his psyche and that was represented only by stereotyped pictures that were like cryptograms of a suffering he had tried to forget.

A Dynasty of Failed Fathers

The next step was very painful for Amos. For a while he dreaded coming to the sessions, because he knew that there was something he had to tell me that he absolutely could not imagine telling me without dying of shame. After weeks of agonizing, he said, "OK, I'll turn around the chair. Don't even dare look at my back. And then I'll tell you."

The horrible secret that he had such difficulty telling me was a memory. He remembered going to sleep in his father's bed when he was five or six years old.. His father would lie with his back to him. Amos remembered being deeply excited by his father's back, which seemed huge to him. What made him shiver now was the recognition that there had been something unmistakably sexual in his excitement.

For weeks Amos felt terrible about even coming to the therapy sessions. He would say with boyish humor (which covered up a genuine sense of being tortured), "You can't expect me to come here and talk about being sexually attracted to my father. It's bad enough to have an Oedipus complex, but *this!!*"

During subsequent sessions, haltingly, and then more fluently, Amos's father began to come into focus. At first Amos regained memories that surprised him and seemed to be in strange opposition to the idea that his father had been an exciting, idealized presence in his childhood.

The parents, together with his paternal grandparents, had emigrated to Israel from South Africa before Amos was born.

The grandfather, a businessman of some success in South Africa, had sold his business before moving to Israel. He was a big man with the erect statue of a professional officer (which, it turned out, he had been during World War II). He had maintained a certain type of clubbiness and radiated Anglo-Saxon ebullience throughout his life.

Amos's father was well built but much slighter than his own father. He also, so it turned out, had no sense at all for business. Amos's grandfather often made fun of his son before others: "Well, my dear son would never have made it in the world of business. No acumen whatsoever. And I guess not the type of balls it takes for real business." Talk like that was accompanied with boisterous laughter, and often the grandfather would slap the father's shoulders with a force that almost made him fall.

In South Africa, tennis had been an important part of community life, and Amos's grandfather had been a good player feared for the brute power of his ground shots. Amos's father, as expected, learned to play tennis as well. He was not bad at it, but he had neither his father's brute strength nor (as it turned out a generation later) his son's animal instinct for covering the net and the feline agility that made it possible to retrieve seemingly lost balls. While Amos was still a child, he saw his father and grandfather on the tennis court. His father was not too bad a player, but he seemed frozen on the court. His grandfather, even though in his early 60s, still had his mighty ground strokes, and he blew his son off the court. He made a point of following each point with boisterous, seemingly amiable, laughter that could be heard all around the tennis center.

Gradually, with great pain, Amos began to recount his memories of the humiliation his father suffered at Amos's grandfather's hands. The father had studied architecture but never took the risk of opening his own office. The grandfather's comment was, "Oh, just as well. He would only end up losing the money I have given him."

When Amos was about five years old, his parents decided to leave the small South African colony and moved closer to Tel Aviv. They saw Amos's grandparents now, but their distance did not help much to change Amos's father's state of mind. At home Amos's father was a bully and a tyrant. His mood was consistently terrible, and he expressed his hostility on his family.

Amos was the prime target of his wrath. "You're so fucking lazy; you'll never get anywhere!" was one of his favorite sentences. If Amos brought good grades from school, his father would look at them skeptically and say, "You must be pretty good at cheating."

Once in a while Amos flew into a terrible fit of rage at his father's injustice and would begin to scream at him hysterically. At first the father would laugh, and then, after a while, he would beat Amos up. Many of these interactions happened when guests or members of the wider family were present. Amos remembered his disbelief, time and again, that everybody would sit there and just watch these scenes of horror, which often ended with his being physically hurt quite badly. The more Amos recalled these scenes, the more he came back to a question that left him aching and feeling deserted: "Where the hell was my mother in all this? Why didn't she ever do a thing to protect me?"

Although Amos's father was a bully at home, he was socially shy. The family had moved away from the Anglo-Saxon colony and had thus escaped the tyrannical presence of the grandfather. But now another problem came into focus: Amos's father's Anglo-Saxon manners, combined with his natural shyness and his unease about himself, made it difficult for him to manage in Israel's boisterous, aggressive culture. Amos remembered with great pain how much of an outsider his father was. From about the age of 19, Amos tried to avoid having his friends meet his father because he was ashamed of him.

Around that time a hypothesis began to form in my mind about the meaning of Amos's strange fixation on body-building magazines. He had said that what really turned him on were images of two body builders posing together and that the only content he could associate with them was that the smaller of the two would win the contest. When the hypothesis seemed more and more consistent with the memories that came up, I told Amos, "I have a hunch. The memories that you have brought up have one consistent theme that runs through various variations: in all of them, one person is humiliated, attacked, or put down by someone who is bigger. Your father was humiliated by his father. You were humiliated by your father.

"It must have been terrible for you to see your father reduced to such shame, and you must have wished that he were big and strong enough to stand up to his own father. Maybe, deep inside, you felt that there was a connection between your father's life-long humiliation and his need to abuse you. So you wished, 'If only my father, the smaller one, could beat the bigger one, his father, then maybe he could be a father to me rather than a sadist who has to put me down.'

"At the same time," I continued, "you must have wished that *you* were strong enough to beat your own father; to make it impossible for him to put you down, degrade you, and hit you.

"But all of this was too painful for you really to remember or feel. So you found a frozen picture that condenses all this into a single image: a smaller body builder winning the showdown against the bigger one."

During the months that followed we would return time and again to this hypothesis. Most important, at some point it linked up to the memory Amos found most difficult to bear, that of his sexual excitement at his father's big body in bed, the memory that had made him feel completely perverse. It did make a lot of sense. When he was a small boy, much of the pain he experienced seemed to have to do with physical size: it was always the bigger one who put the smaller one down.

I told Amos, "I don't think that the core of this excitement has anything to do with sex. Every child needs to be able to admire his father and to feel how wonderful, strong, and knowing he is. Your father let you down time and again. Until now, you have not come up with a single memory of your father's actually functioning as a father. At night, when all you saw was your father's back, those may have been the only moments when you could see your father as grand and exciting. Compared with you, he was big, and you could, at least for a few moments, feel that you had a big and powerful father. Or, I should say, you had a father who could actually *be* a father."

The atmosphere in the session with Amos was mostly warm, and yet somehow distant. Amos's favored tone of voice was one of slight irony. He could be playful and intelligent, but ultimately he kept his distance from his own emotions, as well as from me. Now he seemed on the verge of tears: "You mean that I am not a perverse piece of shit with a rotten sexuality that is worth nothing?" he asked.

"I can't really see what is perverse about a boy's wish to have a father who cares for him and protects him instead of putting him down and abusing him" was all I could say.

This insight into the structure of Amos's frozen sexuality was important, but, as it generally is with the psyche, insight as such was not enough to generate change. But it certainly initiated a process, one in which his frozen psyche gradually began to come alive.

THE THERAPEUTIC RELATIONSHIP: FROM DISEMBODIMENT TO TWINSHIP

Even though, in a sense, Amos had trusted me from early on, there was something vaguely disembodied in the way he experienced me. Emotional closeness seemed an impossibility, so he had turned me into a heartless person. The very idea of my having a body was pretty frightening as well, because he was confused about the various senses of closeness. Liking me and feeling close to me almost automatically meant that there had to be some homosexual desire.

After more than a year of work, Amos's relationship to me gradually began to change. He had been so confused about the relationship between emotional closeness, sexual attraction, and what he experienced as a vague, undefined fear about loss of identity that simple liking and emotional support had been too threatening to be allowed. He felt more relaxed and was less frightened of emotional closeness, even though this process took some time evolve.

At several junctures in the therapy, I saw him with his girlfriend. After one of these meetings, in his next individual session he sat down, nonplussed, looked at me, and said, "My girlfriend tells me that I am blind not to see that you really like me." Puzzled, he continued, "That cannot be. You are a man without a heart. I mean, if you did actually like me, I would even have to face the possibility that I like *you*. . . . Oh my God, enough of these obscenities." He swiveled around in his chair and announced, "I will now look at your library. As far as I am concerned, you are heartless, don't have a body, and that's it." The scene was extremely comical, and I burst out laughing and said, "Don't turn around. I have dematerialized for the time being, and there is no body in my chair."

While Amos's psyche began to unfreeze, he could bear more of my material and emotional existence, but very gradually. One day he looked at me with the mock dismay that served to express what he felt while toning it down. "You have a birthmark on your arm! I *saw* it!" he said. "OK, I did accord you a body. Fine. But you are a Greek statue. You are something between body and non-body. Birthmarks? Who do you think you are? A human being? Cut it out immediately; otherwise I will decide that you have no body whatsoever."

The joking was the expression of an important process. Amos had had to turn himself into an empty shell, because the disappointments and intrusions in his past had been so unbearable. The process of unfreezing his psyche (his sexuality, his emotional life, and his bodily experience) went hand in hand with a gradual belief that the emotional reality of the therapeutic situation could be trusted.

Amos began to experience genuine joy in meeting me. He needed to use fewer and fewer of his witty ways of putting distance between himself and his emotions, and he came to express this joy with pleasure. He would often start sessions by saying, "There's a lot of stuff we have to work on, but the most important thing is just to be here."

This joy went along with an idealizing transference. He felt that he had finally found the ideal father whom he had so sorely missed. Everything about me now seemed admirable to him. He gradually came to believe that I cared about him, and this feeling gave him a strong sense of protection.

He was also convinced that we had very similar casts of mind. He would talk about this commonality with the happiness of a child who says to his dad, "I'm just like you!" When I once pointed out to him that his command of English was a lot better than mine, he was pained. It was as if, at this point, he was not able to accept that he might have abilities superior to mine.

This inability also came to the fore in other respects. Amos at this time reveled in the fact that I was taller than he (even though only by an inch), and he was convinced that I was larger and more powerful than he. Once, when I pointed out to him that, while it might be true that I was physically bigger, he was a much better athlete than I, he had trouble accepting this reality too.

At first I thought that Amos was trying to make sure that I was so strong, physically and mentally, that he could not possibly hurt me. When we investigated this thought, it turned out that he did think that I would be hurt by the very knowledge that, in several respects, his abilities were superior to mine.

It turned out, though, that there was another factor involved: Amos needed me as an idealized figure during this period. It was as if a childlike part of him finally wanted to bask in the experience of a father who was truly admirable. So, for the time being, I did not touch on this aspect of the transference too much. Instead I let Amos enjoy the feeling that he was safe and that he could really enjoy a warm emotional relationship.

UNFREEZING THE PSYCHE

Now Amos began to be inundated with dreams. There were two types of recurring dreams. In one, he was pursued by witches, and the dreams essentially consisted of his running away from the witches. In the second recurring dream, his father humiliated and physically abused him in front of the whole family, and no one even took notice.

The dreams changed crucially after we had done some work on them. He still had some dreams about being pursued by witches, but now he turned back on the witches and fought back. The dreams involving his father changed too: the new recurring dream was that he physically tried to hit and strangle his father, but to no avail. He would lose all his strength, and his attack was as ineffectual as that of a young child hitting an adult.

In the actual relationship with his father, things began to change as well. Once, when his father had denigrated him again, telling him that he did not believe that Amos had ever done anything decent in his life, Amos got up and said, "When you start behaving like anything remotely resembling a father, I'll talk to you again." He would not put up with his father's destructive outbursts anymore. As a result, his father withdrew and began drinking heavily, which, in turn, led to massive pressure from his mother to be nicer to his father.

Episodes like that could make Amos feel unreal again. The family dynamic essentially meant, "If you don't put up with your father's destructiveness, you will end up killing him." We did some work on how he was being pushed back into his shell and feeling dead, and this led to a surprising effect.

One day Amos drove to his parents' house and told his father, "Look, all I ever wanted from you was for you to be a father, to love me. All I ever got was your attempts to undermine me, to tell me what a piece of shit I was. I see no need at all to apologize to you. If anything, I'm willing to forgive you, but only under one condition: I will not take any of your shit anymore, and I demand that you be my *father.*" His father was flabbergasted at first and asked for some time to think things over. Some days later, he called and then came over to Amos's place, where they had a moving encounter. Tearfully, they reaffirmed their bond. It was not to last, as Amos's father very quickly reverted to his sullen destructiveness. But the episode certainly helped Amos to maintain his own sense of reality, and he was not to look back anymore.

Soon he dreamt again that he physically attacked his father, and this time he felt his own physical strength. He subdued his father and let loose. Now he felt—in life as well as in his dreams—that his father could not empty him of his vitality and strength and that, therefore, to his own surprise in his waking life, he would not kill his father in his dreams.

Parallel to this process, Amos began gradually to get to know a sexuality that changed in the very process of becoming known. I have already spoken of the first step, in which the body-building skills acquired a meaning. The next step was that they acquired movement. Amos fantasized scenes in which two men competed against each other, and the erotic high point was when the younger man turned out to be the stronger.

Interestingly enough, there was no sexual activity in any of these fantasies. Knowing that, as long as sex did not appear in his fantasies, it meant that sex was still a matter of fighting for his integrity rather than really allowing himself sexual pleasure, we wondered about this missing sexual activity. Correspondingly, the actual sex he could have with his girlfriend was still infrequent.

The first, momentous step occurred when Amos found himself fantasizing a scene in which a tall, strong woman sexually overwhelmed a smaller man. That content in itself was interesting and even puzzling. In the therapy sessions we would try to figure out the dream. I cannot say that we ever quite got a handle on it, because, while we were speculating whether or not this fantasy was an expression of his childhood wish that his mother protect him from his father, the fantasies that emerged had already changed.

One pleasurable consequence of Amos's reconnecting to his body was that he took up playing tennis again. He did not try to compete at the national level again, but at regional contests he blew his opponents off the court. He would tell me about the immense pleasure he took in feeling his body, alive and kicking, on the court. His serve, while not at the immense speed of his heyday, was fast. What he enjoyed most was his net game. After weekend tournaments, he would often show up with bruises and tell me, with a wide grin, how three times he had thrown himself along the net to return an impossible passing shot. Nevertheless, he also told me, sadly, that he now keenly felt the loss of the athletic career he could have had if it had not disappeared from life in his teens.

AMOS'S THEORY: THE IMPORTANCE OF MENTORING

Amos also regained the use of his remarkable intellectual abilities and was admitted to one of the most prestigious Ph.D. programs in his field in the United States. He visits Israel intermittently to see family and friends, and he generally comes in for a couple of sessions. He gives me updates on what is going on in his life and studies. As there is little work to do, we often end up musing together about all kinds of topics.

Amos is very happy with the outcome of our work. And he has a theory about what made it work. Returning to his theory throughout, he claimed that our intellectual discussions, little asides in which I mused about this or that topic (including psychotherapy), were of no less importance than what I would call the strictly therapeutic work.

In retelling this therapy, I have presented those interludes as ways of giving Amos some reprieve from the often arduous emotional processes he underwent. In other words, I thought of them as pauses in the work rather than as the actual work.

Using self-psychology as a guiding framework, I also conceptualized Amos's relishing the similarities of our mindsets as the reflection of his need for a twinship relationship.

Hence, for quite some time, I did not take seriously Amos's claims that "intellectual mentorship" was as important as other aspects of the therapeutic dialogue. Yet in recent years I have had the experience time and again that it is worth listening carefully to what patients have to say about what is therapeutic in the work. Doing so can, at times, be confusing, because patients may say things that contradict, or at least are not included in, accepted therapeutic lore. But, more often than not, I have found patients' theories to be both challenging and illuminating.

Let me, then, for the sake of exploration, take Amos's theory seriously. His argument is that I am too reductive in claiming that our similarity in intellectual bent primarily served his need for twinship in order to strengthen his fragile sense of self. Some of the thoughts about life, philosophy, the relation between the personal and the impersonal in science, and other topics that we discussed were of great value to him.

The term Amos uses, "intellectual mentor," makes the analyst in me shudder. Haven't we "known" for a century that intellectual processes are superficial? Don't we know that what promotes true change is the analysis of transference (or intersubjective exploration, to use a more contemporary term)?

To return to Amos, when I asked him what particular aspects of my way of thinking had been particularly important to him he mentioned my insistence that autobiography is as much creation as it is uncovering, and that the creation of an autobiography is part of the process of self-creation. My belief is that there is no integrated methodology in psychoanalysis and that in most other fields the idea of such a methodology is a sometimes useful and sometimes harmful fiction. He mentioned my insistence that the different goals of life we adhere to conflict with each other. And, finally, he felt that he had been greatly helped by my expressed belief that human beings have a deep need to feel that they are instrumental in creating who they are and how they live.

His list gave me the distinct sense of being well understood, because these ideas are, indeed, central to my conception of life and therapy. In a sense, Amos's precise understanding of my way of thinking made it a bit easier for me to accept his view of the therapeutic process. It should hardly be surprising that my beliefs deeply influence the way I work. When Amos read my *Individuality, The Impossible Project* (Strenger 1998) he felt that none of it surprised him. "Most of this I have heard in one way or another in our sessions," he said.

Amos's sense that my beliefs and personality were a crucial ingredient of our therapeutic work coincides with my own experience as an analysand. Looking back at the various treatments I have been in, I feel that the main sediment each therapist has left in me is her or his particular mode of being, personality, and view of life. As I have written elsewhere (Strenger 2002a), the moments I felt harmed were those when my analysts tried to interpret my perception of their actual personality traits and feelings as transferences.

Amos's theory of therapeutic change goes beyond the currently accepted idea that the analyst's subjectivity is an essential constituent of the therapeutic relationship. It means that the analyst's thoughts, world view, and modes of thinking are as essential to the process as what we generally call "therapeutic technique."

Amos's theory has very respectable ancestry. Henri Ellenberger (1970 p. 501), in his groundbreaking history of psychodynamic thought, claimed that Freud's greatest achievement was the revival of the Greco-Roman philosophical schools in modernity. The Greco-Roman philosophical schools, as Pierre Hadot (1995) has shown convincingly, were not primarily theoretical enterprises. They were designs of thought that integrated the subject's relation and use to her body, her soul, and her mind into a mode of existence. Those who were willing to be initiated into these modes of thinking studied for prolonged periods of time. Their training included theoretical teaching, instruction in spiritual and mental exercises, and their integration into a community that embodied the ideals of the particular school. The philosophers who taught these modes of thinking of necessity needed long training to acquire the disciplines of the self that they taught.

As Martha Nussbaum (1995) has shown, the Greco-Roman philosophical schools were based on theories that integrated cosmology, philosophical anthropology, and detailed views of the place of human beings in the cosmos. The problem is, of course, that contemporary psychoanalysts do not have such an integrated theory of the universe and humanity's place in it.

If we take the analogy between the Greco-Roman schools and psychoanalysis seriously, we need to ask, what would replace that integrated view of human nature in the therapeutic dialogue? Many contemporary analysts, from Mitchell (1993) to Phillips (1995), do not think that we even have an integrated theory of how the mind works and how human beings develop (and certainly no cosmology to complete our worldview). I think that holding on to some such theory actually can be harmful to patients (Strenger 1997, 2002). It can lead analysts to force their views of life on their patients while rationalizing this imposition as interpretation of resistance.

Given the lack of an integrated theoretical structure, it is not surprising that contemporary analyst like Bollas (1997) and Eigen (1997) call psychoanalysis an aesthetics of existence. This could be defined as an intuitive sense of what it means to live a life worth living. It includes the therapist's existential sense of what gives life meaning, what everything one believes is necessary for a balanced life—sexuality, relationships, professional and financial success, spiritual fulfillment.

The term aesthetic of existence was coined by Foucault in his later years (neither Bollas 1997 nor Eigen 1997 explicitly refers to him). Foucault (1984) argued that the normalizing pressures of society could be counteracted by considering the goal of life not to achieve some "normative maturity," but to structure one's life as a work of art. Since the domain of art (certainly of modern art) is characterized by the celebration of plurality rather than uniformity of style, there is no single ideal of the good life that should be enforced. It also involves what Michel Foucault (1984) called techniques of the self. These are abilities, mental and physical dispositions, that can be acquired through training and by which one tries to shape oneself according to one's preferred aesthetic of existence.

The idea of disciplines of the self could be used to give the concept of psychoanalytic technique an, albeit paradoxically transformed, relevance. When Michael Eigen (1997) says that he sometimes envisages psychoanalytic treatment as a form of exercise room for the psyche, he points in this direction. The patient, in order to form herself according to a particular aesthetic, needs certain abilities, for example, the capacity to tolerate contradictory feelings, or the ability to tolerate thoughts and wishes that do not conform to her moral standards. Unsurprisingly, the analyst needs to have acquired these skills in order to help others to develop them. The techniques of the self and the analyst's mode of being within the therapeutic relationship vary with the aesthetics of existence (for a more extensive treatment, see Strenger 2002 ch 6).

This is reflected in the contemporary psychoanalytic literature. Bollas's (1989) emphasis seems to be on the ability to experience and cherish various aspects of one's psyche and to feel free in the presence of other human beings. Correspondingly. his mode of being in the consulting room is characterized by extensive use of his own selfstates and thc attempt to use his own personal idiom freely in the presence of patients.

Eigen (1998) tries to help his patients to tolerate and enjoy the farther reaches of their souls, including the depths of despair and the exhilaration of spiritual rapture. His detailed therapeutic accounts show how he tries to bear these extremes in himself and how he often communicates his experiences to his patients.

Jessica Benjamin (1995) is particularly attuned to patients' ability to live the complex dialectics of intersubjective recognition. And she is keenly attuned to the ways in which this dialectic can collapse into interactions of dominance and submission. Her accounts show her concern for maintaining the dialectic of recognition in the consulting room, thus enacting in her very way of being what she hopes the patients will acquire.

Stolorow and his intersubjectivist colleagues (1987) are concerned with patients' ability to receive and provide intersubjective nourishment and affirmation. The many case examples of these authors show how they put at the center of their work detailed attunement to patients' needs to be understood and to have their subjective experience.

Neville Symington (1993) explicitly focuses on a patient's commitment to care for others. His theory is that narcissism, the turning of the self into an erotic object, is at the center of all psychopathology. His technique emphasizes the analyst's acts of freedom, which are assertions of the analyst's right not to be enmeshed in the patient's narcissistic use of others.

Post-Jungian James Hillman (1975) is concerned with the individual's ability to let images of an archetypal nature grow and to achieve a transsubjective sense of meaning. Correspondingly, his countenance in the therapeutic situation is far less attuned to the patient's fleeting subjective states than with the imagistic material that emerges, primarily in the patient's dreams. By even reading the patient's dream accounts in the session, he exemplifies in his mode of being that the content of what Jungians call the "objective psyche" is the focus of his attention.

I am not claiming that each of these authors (and the list could, of course, be indefinitely extended) exclusively focus on their favorite dimension while neglecting all others. Nevertheless, it is unrealistic to believe that a therapist's personal predilection, her sense of what constitutes the central dimension of meaning in life, does not crucially influence each and every one of her interventions.

The thoughts I am presenting imply a rapprochement between psychoanalysis and existentialist thought. The specifically psychoanalytic way of mentoring is characterized by constant monitoring of the mentoring process in transferential and intersubjective terms. Psychoanalytic clinicians try to be in touch with the multiple layers in the therapeutic relationship and do not allow themselves to identify with their patients' transferential images. The immense complexity of analytic mentoring is that it requires the constant questioning of where the patient captures something real about the analyst and where previous unconscious organizations of experience color the patient's experience of the analyst. Fortunately the dialogical conceptions of many contemporary approaches often allow this exploration to be conducted in cooperation with the patient, rather than requiring the analyst to "process countertransference" on her own. Intersubjectivism and relational psychoanalysis have repeatedly demonstrated how fruitful such exploratory dialogue can be.

The epistemological self-reflection of psychoanalysis in the last two decades demands that we admit that what we offer our patients is not some grand truth about human nature and how to live life, but just an aesthetic of existence. Hence analytic interventions of all sorts can be presented only as thoughts, suggestions, or associations, and only very rarely (as in the diagnosis of psychopathologies that require medication) as authoritative statements. This is probably the best way to avoid the confusion of mentoring with guru status. In analytic terms, the analytic scrutiny of the process prevents the analyst's identification with the patient's idealizing transference.

PRACTICAL IMPLICATIONS: WHO CAN WORK WITH WHOM?

These thoughts have some unsettling byproducts. Psychotherapy and psychoanalysis are supposed to be professions. Hence we would like to think that there is such a thing as a correct technique that determines the outcome of therapy. If Amos's theory is right, there are contingent factors that play a much more dominant role in the success of therapies. If my personality and intellectual bent had been less akin to Amos's, would the therapy have been less successful?

I believe that such was actually the case. With Amos, the result was beneficial, but it is often painful for me to realize that I am less effective as a therapist with patients with whom I have less an affinity than with Amos and whose abilities and personality traits are less easy for me to celebrate. This idea is consistent with thoughts I have already developed about what the analyst brings into the therapeutic relationship. An aesthetic of existence is, after all, an intensely personal issue. The relative weight the analyst places on the various facets of existence is, in my view, not something that can (or should) be ignored.

The patient also brings an aesthetic of existence (a personal idiom, to use Bollas's [1989] term) to the therapeutic relationship. If the goal of the analytic encounter is to enable the patient to bring her own aesthetic of existence to full expression, it must be taken into account that the analyst's personal idiom may or may not be congenial to the patient's and suitable for therapeutic use. The fit between the two personalities depends, after all, on both participants in the dyad.

A practical implication of these thoughts is that we need to rethink our policies about who can work with whom. If the main ingredient of the therapeutic process is a personal relationship, no technique can overcome the analyst's temperamental traits.

It is my sense that, despite the intense preoccupation with the analyst's subjectivity, the current literature is still underestimating the extent to which patients read our actual states of mind. In particular, they feel the extent to which we cherish who they are. Analytic schools that emphasize long-term working within a negative transference (Schafer 1997) may simply be providing a rationalization for continuing treatments that are doomed to be fruitless.

This idea squares with one of the most consistently replicated findings in psychotherapy research (Orbach and Simons 1991; Orlensky, Grawe, and Park 1994; Orbach and Greenberg 2000). That is, that the quality of the therapeutic relationship at the beginning of treatment is one of the best predictors of therapeutic success. Hence we may be doing our patients a disservice by trying to stretch our range of therapeutic abilities beyond the limits set by our basic character structures.

I am not implying that training and professional and personal maturity cannot broaden the range of patients that we can relate to, work with (Strenger 1997, 2002), and cherish as human beings. But the reversal of emphasis from technique to personal relationship that I propose puts into question how much technique (including the constant monitoring and analyzing of countertransference) can mitigate personal predilections and aversions.

If the analyst's personality is an ineradicable factor in the therapeutic encounter, we cannot continue to assume that countertransference can always be kept in check, let alone be neutralized. The very term countertransference originally implied a neurotic reaction to a patient and in some contemporary uses refers to the analyst's reactions to the patient's wishes and desires (Gorkin 1987). If, instead, we take into account that there are human reactions to another human being that are simply expressions of the analyst's basic personality, our perspective may change. It may just not be true that every analyst can work with every patient, not because the analyst is insufficiently analyzed, but because (as in every human relationship) it is sometimes not possible to link two unique personalities into a fruitful relationship.

A practical consequence of such thoughts would be that analysts would have to do some soul searching about what type of patients they are effective with and what kind of patients they cannot fruitfully engage with. In the course of their careers, analysts should acquire a sense of their strengths and limitations. Once these limitations are not necessarily considered to be either signs of insufficient personal analysis or indications of psychopathology, we can look at them differently. The very same character traits that make a particular analyst useful for some patients may make it more difficult for her to work with other patients. It would, therefore. be professionally and ethically preferable to refer patients whom one has difficulty cherishing to colleagues who may be temperamentally more inclined to react to those patients positively.

A final remark: in this chapter I explore a train of thought and push it to its ultimate logical conclusion. It has some problematic consequences: are there not quite a few patients who are, almost by their very nature, "unwanted patients" (Eigen 1993 ch 4)? Who, in the conception I am proposing, should be working with them? Where is the boundary between awareness of one's strengths and weaknesses and simply trying to take life easy?

There also is a voice inside me that insists that there is indeed something like therapeutic technique, at which in due time we become better; for example, letting potential space evolve and realizing that there are better as well as less fruitful ways of handling transferential entanglements. I offer these thoughts for consideration not so much as unshakeable convictions but as a reconceptualization that, even if it turns out to be exaggerated, might contribute to a deeper understanding of what transpires in our consulting rooms.

Another implication that needs some rethinking is that this strategy may have unwelcome financial implications. There may be periods in an analyst's practice when few people who suit her personal aesthetic turn to her or him. Can we seriously demand that analysts refrain from taking on patients who do not suit them?

I cannot say that I have easy answers to this and other questions. But my hunch is that the profession might be ready for new approaches. Therapists talk informally to and about each other a great deal. From personal acquaintance or through the grapevine of the profession, we often have a pretty clear sense of who is good at working with what type of patient. Nina Coltart (1996) made such knowledge into a vocation: apart from her own practice, she is said to have seen more than 3000 patients for intakes to refer them elsewhere.

I have adopted this strategy and have had positive experiences with it. Whenever patients ask for my help, I see them for a few sessions to find out how well we connect. I invite them to share their gut feeling about their encounters with me, and I tell them when I think I may not be the right person to work with them. In the majority of cases, the feelings (both positive and negative) are remarkably mutual, as they often are in ordinary life.

Of course, this approach, like any other, is not without its problems. Patients may feel that they are in some kind of audition, that they must please or be impressive in order to be accepted for therapy. As a result. they may be more attuned to cues to what induces interest or liking in the therapist rather than communicating authentically.

I have found, though, that patients react favorably and productively to a truly open explanation for the rationale of the procedure. I tell them that entering therapy or analysis is a huge investment, existentially, mentally, and financially, and that the fit between patient and analyst is a crucial determinant of outcome. I explicitly tell them that this interview might be misconstrued as an entrance exam, but it is really an attempt to optimize help for them.

I have no illusions that such an explanation precludes all possibility of the patients' interpreting it in terms of earlier experiences. They may hear it as a threat of rejection or as an invitation to impress or to seduce. Nevertheless, by and large, my experience has been positive: most patients accept the invitation for a mutual exploration of fit. And I have also found that, if we come to the conclusion that they need someone else, they will think, together with me, about what type of therapeutic style and personality would suit them best.

In the few cases in which patients felt they wanted to stay on, when I felt differently, some a priori transference (generated through excessively positive recommendation, previous reading, or other factors) seemed to make them less responsive to their own visceral reactions to me. While this possibility cannot be denied, I still think that trying to find out whether a particular potential therapeutic dyad is viable is vastly preferable to embarking on a therapeutic journey that is not likely to succeed.

By building a network of colleagues whom I know well, I can refer patients with whom I tend to be less effective to colleagues who I have reason to believe will be more congenial to these patients. If we get to the point of accepting that our own personality, with its strengths and weaknesses, honed by experience, training, and theoretical knowledge, is the main tool that we have to offer to our patients, we might go one step further and integrate informal knowledge into the profession's explicit discourse.

Chapter 5

Finding Ethnic Identity and A Place in Western Society

What is it like to be born into an ethnic group that is considered second rate by the dominant culture in the country of origin? What is it like to consolidate a sense of self and identity when one's parents are dejected and uprooted? What are the psychological consequences of the quandary between loyalty to one's family and the distinct sense that one needs to break out of the confines of one's upbringing?

In the age of the politics of identity and political correctness, it has become a matter of course for most of us that ethnic identities are to be respected. It has also become an anathema for many to argue for the superiority of Western culture. Yet such taboos may often prevent us from seeing what individual experiences are like.

For many people who belong to ethnic minorities, Western culture is not necessarily the oppressor; it is often experienced as a wide space of liberation. What can turn the fates of these people into almost irresolvable tragedies is that the very same culture that they experience as liberating also may have inflicted horrible pain on them, their families, and their ethnic group. The almost inevitable result is that they experience themselves as irredeemably damaged.

The difficulties of negotiating ethnic identity with finding a place in Western society are pervasive. In the United States, Latinos, ethnic Chinese, and many other groups live with this predicament. In Western Europe it is the daily plight of immigrants from Eastern Europe, and even more so of immigrants from various Muslim countries who try to find their place in their new environment (Akhtar 1999).

In Israel, where I live and work, this tension is palpable and dramatic, particularly because it involves so many disparate groups: Jewish immigrants from Arab countries and from the former Soviet Republics. And, of course, there is the terrible dilemma of loyalty of Israel's Muslim Arab citizens. Yet, despite the particular intricacies of the Israeli context, some of the themes in the story to be told are to be found in other areas of the world as well.

The Psychoanalytic Consulting Room as a Microcosm

The difficulty of identifying with the culture that has condemned one to second-rate status is brought into sharp focus in the prism of the psychotherapeutic consulting room. In this chapter, I speak of the treatment of a woman of Moroccan origins. Ruth, in her 30s, specifically sought out me, a member of what is considered the "dominant" group in her country of origin, to heal the wounds of her self-experience. My identity as an Ashkenazi intellectual was the explicit reason she chose to seek help from me.

This treatment, like any other treatment of considerable length and depth, has many facets and aspects. I would like to focus on the wounds generated by Ruth's long and arduous journey into the mainstream of Israeli society. I believe that in her treatment the social reality of a society in turmoil was reflected in the microcosm of the consulting room and in our interactions and entanglements. This is, to some extent, true of any analytic treatment, but this treatment may highlight the extent to which the social and political realms permeate the psyche of each individual.

The psychoanalytic consulting room became a microcosm that reflected a wider social, historical, cultural, and political reality. Some background material is, I believe, important for understanding the intersubjective reality of this treatment.

As has been amply documented (Avineri 1980; Shapira 1997), the Zionist movement and the State of Israel were based on the idea that a new type of Jew had to be created. The New Jew was supposed to be the opposite of what was perceived as the Old Jew of Eastern Europe. Whereas the Old Jew was powerless, oppressed, often subservient, and frightened, the New Jew was supposed to be assertive, belligerent, able to defend himself, and proud of his strength.

The emotional charge of the image of the Old Jew has been an overwhelmingly threatening force after the horrors of the Holocaust in which six million Jews were murdered. The State of Israel came into being against the background of the Holocaust, which proved that it was indeed imperative for Jews to have a homeland of their own. The image of the Old Jews who could be brought to the slaughterhouse like sheep (a prevalent metaphor in Israeli collective memory, as Shapira 1997 has shown), reinforced the fear that, indeed, the Old Jew was a constant threat to the identity of the New Jew. The first generation of Israelis was not willing to hear of the Holocaust. Their sense of a new identity was too threatened by dealing with the helplessness of Jews during the Holocaust.

After the successful defense of the new state against the combined attack of a number of neighboring countries, it was imperative to increase the Jewish population if Israel was to stand a chance of surviving. Parallel to this need, the situation of Jews in Arab countries began to deteriorate, as Arab collective identity began to coalesce around rejection of Israel's existence.

In the 1950s more than one million Jews emigrated to Israel from Arab states, including Algeria, Morocco, Tunisia, Yemen, Iraq, and Iran. A large part of this immigration was sponsored by state agencies like the Jewish Agency, and within a few successive years Israel more than doubled its population. The fledgling state's means to integrate this immigration were limited. Many of the immigrants (including many Jews from Ashkenazi background, such as a large Romanian contingent), spent their first years in asbestos huts in less than habitable conditions before they were offered permanent housing.

Nevertheless there is truth in the sometimes distorted but well-documented fact that Sephardic Jews from North African countries (Iran, Iraq, and Syria) underwent a particularly difficult process of absorption. One repeated pattern has become part of Israeli lore: many Sephardic Jews, on disembarking from the ships that brought them to the port of Haifa, were immediately treated with DDT. There was an unspoken assumption that they were hygienically unsound and needed to be disinfected.

The DDT episode is the tip of the iceberg composed of a deeper trend in the absorption of Sephardic Jewry. The Eastern European establishment, with its socialist-progressive ideology, assumed that Jews of Arab background came from primitive cultural roots that were not worth preserving. Sephardic Jews were predominantly traditional with respect to religion, whereas the dominant Zionist ethos was secular. The predominant view was that the state needed to take a paternalist view toward Sephardic immigrants, strip them of their backward culture, and imbue them with the new Zionist ethos.

The result was that many of the first generation Sephardic immigrants suffered traumatic and humiliating experiences. Some of them, particularly those of Iraqi background, had enjoyed decent middle-class status in their countries of origin; they had been small entrepreneurs, teachers, or civil servants. None of their credentials were taken to be of value by the Israeli state, and most of them suffered devastating losses of status and respectability. Others had been led to expect that the land of milk and honey would take care of their needs and that they were entitled to be taken care of by the Zionist state (this expectation having been reinforced by what they had been told by government agencies), only to find out that an inept and often insensitive bureaucracy had neither the financial nor the human resources to meet their needs.

The combination of lack of funds and lack of respect for their culture of origin disenfranchised many of the first-generation Sephardic immigrants. They found themselves stripped of self-respect and categorized as second-rate citizens. That they were recognizable physically by their darker Middle Eastern complexions gave this stereotyping a racial tinge that would very quickly become part of Israeli culture.

In no time, Israel had evolved a class stratification. Its structure was atypical because it was not primarily based on material wealth. The aristocracy was composed of European Jews who had arrived in Israel before the establishment of the state and their children. In the 50s and 60s, a generation came of age that was already Israeli born. The *Sabras,* as they were called, were proud of their provenance. They were the prime specimens of the New Jew: tough, plain spoken, belligerent, proof that indeed the experiment of creating the New Jew had succeeded. The military successes of 1948, 1956, and 1967 gave the myth of the New Jew historical validity and international recognition.

Sephardic Jews mostly did not partake of this new, proud identity. The first generation of Israeli-born Sephardic Jews grew into the reality of being categorized as second rate. Most of them saw their parents destitute, devoid of self-respect and social standing. Many of them were torn between the keen desire to make their way in an Ashkenazi-dominated society and preserving their ethnic identity. The politics of Sephardic identity emerged only gradually. It was to take decades until some of them acquired prominence in the three domains that defined the Israeli social hierarchy: the political, military, and business elites. It was a long time until there were recognizably Sephardic generals and major politicians.

I propose that the treatment of Sephardic Jews in Israel was the result of an uncanny return of the repressed. The image of the Old Jew—dejected, oppressed, ridiculed, and powerless—continued to loom large in the unconscious of the New Jew. Sephardic Jews, for reasons to be elaborated later, were ideally suited to the projection of the image of the Old Jew.

Before embarking on the tale of Ruth's therapeutic journey, I would like to make a cautionary statement. I have capitalized the terms Old Jew and New Jew, and throughout this chapter I make ample reference to "the Ashkenazi Elite," "typical Israeli male," and "Sephardic Jews." In so doing, I do not intend to reify the stereotypes I am using. Neither do I believe in the existence of a monolithic Old Jew or that the New Jew is a *creation ex nihilo.* Nor do I believe in the existence of "the Ashkenazi" or "the Sephardic" Jew as a genetic, cultural, or social entity. These references are meant to denote images that are prevalent in Israeli society and have powerful psychic impact.

I would like to thank Ruth for her cooperation and help in writing this chapter. She was generous in sending me notes that she had made during the course of this treatment (which ended several years ago) and her current thoughts and feelings about her therapeutic journey. She has read and endorsed the final version of this chapter and feels that it reflects the essence of both her biography and our common journey. I have made every effort to disguise her identity. While preserving the central psychic, existential, and therapeutic processes, I have, with her help, crafted a biography that eliminates every identifying detail.

A Hypothesis

I myself was neither born nor raised in Israel. It took me years to decipher the codes of Israeli society, and I have always retained my European identity. I think that I truly came to understand the depths of the Sephardic predicament in the psychotherapeutic consulting room.

From the mid-80s, during my training in Jerusalem, and from the late 1980s onward, when I went into private practice in Tel Aviv, I have treated many Sephardic Jews. Some of them had to their credit enormous achievements ranging from the building of business empires, through literary accomplishments (e.g., Strenger 1998 ch 9), or academic work. All of them, consistently, despite considerable variation in life histories, temperamental propensities, gender, age, and family status, carried enormous pain inside themselves.

What strikes me is the consistency with which they reported dreams about their bodies being filled with worms, cockroaches, or filth. None of them had any formally diagnosable psychopathology that could explain this recurrent theme.

The hypothesis that I have come to entertain is that it is not just the vile treatment of the generation of their parents that created this deeply wounded self-image of being filthy to the core. I suspect that Israeli society has tended to project disowned aspects of its identity connected to the Old Jew onto the Sephardic population. Hence, in addition to the particular biographies of individual patients, they seem to be, collectively, the recipients of these projections.

I am a male Ashkenazi Jew and thus a representative of the group that has inflicted the collective wounds onto Sephardic Jewry. In therapeutic work with Sephardic Jews this creates highly complex intersubjective dynamics. Elsewhere (Strenger 1998 ch 9) I have reported one such treatment, in which my identity as an Ashkenazi academic and intellectual received a particular transferential color. For that young man, recognition of his value as a human being by an Ashkenazi academic was a way to heal some of the wounds in his identity, and to find his own voice and creativity.

RUTH: THE FIRST SESSION

Ruth told me over the phone that she had heard me speak at some event. Her voice became hesitant. Did I have a vacancy? When I answered in the affirmative, there was a sigh of relief, and we fixed an appointment.

When I opened the door, I saw a young woman in her 30s. Her skin color was dark (by Israeli standards), and yet somehow she looked pale. I noticed that she wore a relatively formal dress that was buttoned up to her throat.

We sat down in my consulting room. Ruth cleared her throat. She had trouble speaking. Her voice trembling, she finally said, "I chose you. You have to understand; this is very special to me. I was scared to death you would tell me you have no time. Or that you only take on certain patients."

Ruth was completely overwhelmed with emotion. She was literally shaking now, sitting upright, not using the backrest. I asked her if she could explain to me what she meant by having chosen me. She tried to speak, her chest heaving, but, instead of speaking, she was shaken by heavy sobs. Tears were streaming down her face. Thus began what would turn out to be a difficult and yet rewarding journey that was to teach me a great deal about the pains of growing up as a member of an ethnic group that is considered second rate in the society you live in, and about my own difficulty living with the guilt of belonging to the ethnic group categorized as the elite.

Once Ruth had calmed down, she began to apologize for her outburst. Under most circumstances, I would have been worried by such a dramatic opening. I would have wondered if a patient who could not adhere to the ritual of introducing herself to the therapist was going to be too difficult to handle. Yet I felt strangely moved by Ruth's outburst. I experienced her as a child who had waited too long to arrive at a safe haven and who could not contain both the excitement and the relief of finally having made it home. Home? Why did I think of our sessions in these terms?

I told Ruth that she should not feel uncomfortable, that I was fine with her crying. When she finally was able to speak, she said, "On stage you were this wide-ranging intellectual. You spoke with such conviction and self-confidence; yet there was a lot of feeling there. You stood for all that I admired.

"And yet, during the break, you were mostly by yourself. I had the distinct feeling that you felt uncomfortable when people approached you and complimented you on your lecture. Fiddling with your jacket, you accepted the compliments with a somewhat frozen smile. It seemed to me that you wanted to get out of there as quickly as possible. Despite your radiance on the podium, once you were among people, you looked like a stranger, someone who did not feel at home among his colleagues.

"I was watching you all the time. And during the break I felt close to you. I could identify with your discomfort. Behind your charisma, you are really shy. It was during this break that I decided that I wanted you as a therapist."

I was both touched and taken aback by Ruth's analysis. Indeed, I often feel uncomfortable after my lectures. Instead of being able to enjoy expressions of enthusiasm and gratitude (if the lecture was any good)– even though I cherish them–I often feel at a loss to know how to react.

How had she picked up all that? I thought I was pretty good at hiding my discomfort and that my persona was relatively free of cracks at the time. If anything, I was afraid that, by trying to hide a core of shyness, I was using too much cockiness as a cover-up. Yet I felt less found out and invaded than understood and seen.

Ruth continued, "I wanted to be in treatment with this man who had such breadth and a good deal of show-talent, and yet was so unsure of himself. I felt that you would be able to give me all I needed to fill the void that had accumulated in my life."

A Difficult Life Trajectory

Ruth, the first of five children, was born in Tel Aviv into a Moroccan family. Her father was a small shopkeeper; her mother, to this very day, cleans homes to help make ends meet. They lived in a poor neighborhood in southern Tel Aviv.

Until the age of 12, Ruth defined her horizon by their neighborhood. She had been taken to the north of Tel Aviv, where the better-to-do, mostly Ashkenazi middle and upper middle classes lived.

Her home neighborhood was clean, orderly, and free of crime. But it was filled with poverty and permeated with an aura of only limited possibilities. Her father, who had been a teacher back in Morocco, did not have the credentials to pursue his profession in Israel. Consequently, he had opened the little grocery shop because he needed to try to earn a living. But the downgrade in status had broken something in him. Ruth did not remember a time when her father was not an alcoholic. Most days when he came home he would start drinking.

Ruth explained, "He was not what you expect of an alcoholic. He was neither violent nor abusive. He was a very mild-mannered man. From his home he had brought a culture of reading and a connection to Jewish tradition. He was not the type to raise a hand against anyone. But his spirit was broken. It may sound strange to you, but, in his own way, my father is an intellectual. But no one recognizes it."

Ruth's voice was trembling. The memory of her father's humiliation was too much to bear. I felt torn. I could sense how she was trying desperately to maintain something of her father's honor and dignity. To this very day her descriptions of her father's rantings at home make me feel as if I had been present to hear them. I could sense this little man's outrage at his fate, his helplessness in a society that refused to give him any recognition, his humiliation at being seen by his wife and children in states of stupor and loss of control.

I could also feel what must have gone through the little girl's mind as she watched her father's misery. She needed to love and admire him, and instead she was faced with his despondency and his need to run away from his own unbearable humiliation. In the young girl's mind this humiliation was somehow connected to their ethnic provenance. Her brief forays into northern Tel Aviv had brought her to the conclusion that her family's darker complexion must be at the root of her father's humiliation.

Her mother was a beloved figure in the neighborhood. Her kitchen was a hub of information and personal communication.

People came to her for advice, for food, for support. She contributed to the family's meager income not only by cleaning homes but also by laundering fabrics that needed special care.

Yet, even though Ruth's mother was charismatic and beloved, she carried horrible anxieties in her soul. Her family had lived in one of the rural areas of Morocco. On the trip to the seaport where they would leave the country and go to Israel, several of her family members died. She arrived in Israel still a child, with no one to guide and support her. From the age of 10 she worked to support her family. Ruth's mother seldom spoke of the horrors of her journey to Israel and the losses she had incurred. She also rarely complained of having missed out on the opportunity to get an education (she was practically illiterate). Yet on many occasions Ruth sensed that her mother was filled with anxious apprehension. Her mother always seemed to be waiting for the next catastrophe to arrive. The slightest problem within the family would send her into fits of anger, crying, and helplessness.

Ruth remembered her parents as always overburdened with life. They had no inclination or ability to relate to their children as individuals. She and her siblings were "children" to be raised and somehow brought through life. Ruth's father clung to the last vestiges of his original identity by insisting on a traditional Jewish life style.

Ruth's earliest memories gravitated to a child's dim awareness that somewhere, in the north of town, there was a better life; there were people who dressed more nicely, seemed to be at ease with themselves, had cars, spoke a nicer language. And their skin color was lighter than hers.

One day her mother came home and saw Ruth in the bathtub with a bottle of bleach in her hand. Alarmed, she asked Ruth what she was doing. Ruth simply explained to her that she wanted to wash off her dark skin color, so she would be white like the people she had seen in the beautiful areas of northern Tel Aviv.

At age six Ruth wanted to take ballet classes, but her parents did not have the money for either the shoes and clothes or for the tuition. So, despite the teacher's invitation, she did not show up for the first class. When the teacher asked her why, she explained that her parents could not pay for either the tuition or the outfits. The ballet teacher, moved by the little girl's plight, helped her out, and Ruth was to participate in classes for two years. After that, her father intervened: in his eyes his daughter was baring herself to the male gaze, and this was not acceptable.

Nevertheless the experience with the ballet teacher proved pivotal. Throughout her childhood and adolescence, Ruth had several teachers who recognized her potential and tried to help her to move out of her confining circumstances. There was something in Ruth that mobilized potential mentors to help her. Ruth became special to them, and they invested time and energy in her. Through her mentors' eyes, she could see what she had been yearning for but had never received from her parents: recognition of her individuality as valuable.

As part of a social project, Ruth was one of a group of students from her neighborhood chosen to attend high school in the well-to-do north of Tel Aviv. So, at age 14, she finally moved into the wide world that she had seen from afar during her family's rare outings into the world of Ashkenazi Jews. Ruth felt proud, yet disoriented and afraid. Was she going to be able to fulfill the expectations of her?

Again her natural propensity to attract mentors helped. One of her high-school teachers took on the task of helping the dark-skinned girl with the wide, slightly scared, and yet inquisitive eyes. Thus Ruth managed to graduate from high school, served in the army, and then began to study social sciences at the university. In her mid-20s, in the midst of her university studies, Ruth met Alain, an attaché to the French embassy. He almost immediately fell in love with her exotic beauty and the fierce intensity of her emotional expression. It seems that something in his personality also responded to her desperate need for someone to help her in consolidating her still shaky self-esteem.

She fell in love with his integrity, good looks, class, culture, and calm self-assurance. She also soon came to cherish his generosity, devotion, and capacity for emotional sustenance. After about a year, they were married. They had two children, a son and a daughter, and Ruth was a devoted mother and spouse. Nevertheless, she continued to suffer from bouts of deep depression. She sought treatment several times, but still felt that the core of her emotional problems had remained untouched.

STAGES OF A THERAPEUTIC JOURNEY

At the beginning of the treatment, Ruth told me about an experience that was to become a central metaphor throughout our journey. "I once took a tour in the Negev [the desert in the south of Israel]. The tour guide was this really good-looking guy. An Ashkenazi with black curly hair, tanned, athletic, well built, and a real charmer. One day we had a pretty rocky ride with the Jeep, and I felt that I was going to throw up. I asked the guide to stop, jumped out of the Jeep, ran behind it, and in three huge upheavals emptied my stomach. When I turned around, I almost fainted. The tour guide was standing right behind me and watching me intently. I wanted to die. It was so important for me to be attractive to him, and here he had seen me in one of the most unappetizing situations on earth.

"I screamed at him, 'Why did you watch?' He looked at me with a gaze full of love and desire and said. ' If you want me to, I'll eat your puke.' I saw in his eyes that he meant it. Finally I felt clean. I felt that my insides. which I had hated all my life, might not be as disgusting as I had always thought."

Ruth began to cry. Her eyes were examining my facial expression. Her voice was trembling when she asked me, "Could you eat my puke, Carlo? Could you?" She would soon express this need for acceptance in other ways.

After about a year into our work, Ruth went through one of the most difficult sessions in what had already been an emotionally difficult process. On the face of it, the event she described was not wrenchingly painful compared with other facets of her life. She told me that in her childhood there was not enough money in the family to buy reserve underwear, and, since her mother was working so hard and long, she did not always have the time to wash the children's underwear. As a result, Ruth often found herself with panties that were not completely clean.

I had seen Ruth crying her heart out before. But in this session her sobs shook her to the core. I was almost frightened by the intensity of her crying and the immense pain and humiliation she experienced while relating this memory.

Ruth and I were to discuss this session time and again in the latter course of our journey. The soiled panties acquired many symbolic meanings. They meant that Ruth always felt that there was something filthy that she had to hide. The dark stains symbolized the color of her skin, which was different from the lighter shades of the ruling classes, and the dark secret of her father's alcoholism and humiliation. The intensity of her pain can be understood only against the background of her feelings, which expressed themselves in a series of dreams. In one of the dreams, worms were crawling out of her legs; in others, there was uncontrollable defecation, either by her or by a baby of hers.

But, more than anything, the very act of letting me into her soiled underpants, as she once put it, was of significance. Telling me of the shame that she had felt and expressing the depth of her despair was the therapeutic analogue to throwing up near the tour guide. At the time of this episode, her love for me was probably at its greatest intensity. Nothing mattered more than what I felt about her, whether I accepted and cherished her and found her attractive.

To tell me about her soiled underpants in the midst of all this was to take a high emotional risk. It meant that she hoped to cleanse herself of the feeling of being stained that had led the six-year-old to want to bleach the color of her skin. For Ruth, it was the analogue to the question that she had asked me before: "Could you eat my puke?"

The Depths of Transference Love

Ruth began to feel that she had been incredibly lucky with her choice of therapist. She felt uniquely understood and idealized many aspects of who I was—ranging from my style of clothing to my intellectual interests. And she developed a deep erotic attachment to me. She often dreamt about erotic encounters with me and entertained conscious fantasies about them.

There was an interesting disparity between these fantasies and other aspects of Ruth's experience of me. On one hand, she would often emphasize that she experienced me as quintessentially male. She would speak of my style of dressing, which at the time was composed mostly of jeans and boots. On the other hand, her erotic fantasies had none of the phallic character that she ascribed to my appearance. In those fantasies, our erotic encounter was primarily about being at one with another. She often said, "In my fantasies, making love to you would almost be like making love to a woman. I always imagine that you would feel me from inside as no man possibly could."

Some of the time I felt capable of relating appropriately both to the idealization and the erotization. I saw them as the expression of a profound need to repair her damaged self-experience. I assumed that her yearning for my erotic acceptance was an attempt to heal this damage by merging with an idealized man. If I could desire and cherish her, she might begin to feel that the core of her self was not ill and rotten as her dreams showed.

For a prolonged period, I felt quite comfortable with this idealization and the sexual content of Ruth's wishes. The warm, erotic atmosphere fueled the therapeutic process with emotional energy. Ruth is a beautiful woman, and I found her attractive. We could freely explore the meanings of her erotic fantasies, and I was optimistic about the treatment's course.

Yet things turned out to be more complicated than I expected. Ruth more and more spoke of the artificiality of therapeutic boundaries. "If we had met under different circumstances, we might have had an affair. So what if I have met you as a therapist?" Feeling accused and on the defensive, I sometimes tried to reason with her. I would say something like, "Ruth, fate has brought us together as patient and therapist. In fact, you *chose* me to be your therapist. Now we need to give meaning to our encounter within this context." Such utterances did, of course, not get us far. Instead, Ruth's insistence on the possibility of an erotic encounter acquired the character of a moral demand. It was as if, by having accepted the role of therapist, I now *owed* her the erotic encounter that, so she felt, would heal her damaged self.

I had moments of impatience when I confronted her with the unrealistic nature of her desires and encouraged her to explore the motives behind both the erotization and the idealization. Strangely enough, I did so against my own better judgment: in general I tend to accept Kohut's (1971) hypothesis that transferential idealization is mostly the expression of an unmet developmental need—and in Ruth's case I had reasonable hypotheses about the historical roots of these unmet selfobject needs.

I lost my bearings more than once with Ruth and actually became angry with her and demanded that she be a more cooperative patient. I have wondered why and have come to a conclusion about one of the origins of this difficulty of mine. Every psychoanalytic consulting room is, of necessity, located in a particular political and cultural space. In Lacanian (1977) terms, the Other permeates the consulting room just as it does any other space. My position in the consulting room was doubly loaded with difficulty. Not only was I the representative of the dominant, Ashkenazi culture. I was also a member of the gender that dominates Israel. As such, I was, by virtue of gender and ethnic provenance, doomed to be guilty and obligated to make reparation. I was one of those born into an advantaged class, and one of a gender that has dominated women throughout history.

Something in me profoundly refused to accept this historical collective guilt. Both as a man and as a therapist, I have experienced many moments of outrage about having to pay for an oppressive role I have taken pains to avoid in my life. To this I must add an additional complexity: not being Israeli born and having grown up as a Jew in Switzerland, I have myself experienced what it is like to be part of a minority. My refusal to identify fully with the male Ashkenazi elite also has to do with my unwillingness to give up my European identity.

The differentiation between Ashkenazi and Sephardic Jewry was not a part of my upbringing. In fact, on arriving in Israel in my early 20s, I had no understanding of this issue whatsoever. This internal Jewish racism was something that I "learned" during my years here. To my horror, I noticed after some years that unconsciously I had begun to internalize the stereotypes of Israeli society. It has taken me years to acknowledge that I have taken on some of the characteristics of this group that I consciously repudiated. And it has taken me more years to find my own voice within a force field of collective identities and the pressure to conform to them (Strenger 2002).

In my adamant fight against being engulfed in an identity that I repudiated in many ways, I now think that I was often on the defensive. Instead of listening to Ruth's feelings from her vantage point, I experienced them as personal accusations and reacted correspondingly. It was as if I were telling her, "Stop classifying me as something I am not." Nevertheless, I am both Ashkenazi and male.

Fortunately Ruth was adamant in her unwillingness to accept my empathic failures. Whenever she felt that I did not understand her, she would angrily confront me with my mistakes. To this day I am grateful to her for her insistence; she forced (and helped) me to provide her with the type of understanding she needed and restored my faith in the power of patient exploration even of intense erotic transferences.

Gradually my ability to work calmly with Ruth's erotic transferences was restored, I became more capable of differentiating between my fears of being an accused male and the true content of Ruth's wishes, and these insights made possible fruitful work on the deeper meanings of her erotic wishes. In particular, as she once put it, I began to realize that Ruth did not think of me as a male who owed her something. Instead she was yearning for me to be a man/woman who would merge with her erotically and psychically. Ruth wanted me to be an Ashkenazi man who could truly sense and feel a Sephardic woman from inside.

The less defensive I became, the more Ruth's erotic wishes lost their aggressive, demanding character. They turned into intense, painful yearnings. The more closely we listened to this quality, the more, to my surprise, a completely new element began to emerge. In her fantasies, my erotic presence had a soothing character. I provided not only pleasure, but also calmness and solace.

Ruth was flooded with memories of how anxious her mother had been. Owing to her own traumas, her mother was constantly waiting for new catastrophes to occur. When Ruth was afraid, her mother could not calm her down and would herself become frantic with anxiety. Ruth was left with a free-floating anxiety that roamed through her soul. Thus erotic union with me was not only a source of the tranquility that she had never experienced, but also a source of acceptance and pleasure.

TOWARD RESOLUTION, HEALING, AND INDIVIDUATION

Despite some fruitful work, Ruth continued to be obsessed with my cherishing her and finding her attractive. Time and again we went through various attempts to understand the function of this need for love. Gradually those attempts took on a repetitive character. At some point, when I felt that we were not making any headway, I took a calculated risk. I felt that Ruth had somehow entrenched herself in the position of endless vulnerability. I was of necessity the abuser. I could never get it right. If I patiently tried to analyze her feelings, I was heartless and distant. If I spoke of my experience of working with her, I failed her and was not sufficiently attentive.

And time and again she resorted to asking me why I excluded the possibility of having sex with her. My sense was that Ruth was perpetuating a theme that she had overcome already. I said, "Ruth, I will ask you a question, and I want an honest answer from you. Imagine that I told you that you were right, that my insistence on not having sex with you was stupid, and that I invited you to my bedroom. What would you feel and what would you do?"

Ruth looked at me intently and thought about my question for a minute or two. Then she looked at me earnestly and said, "I would grab my stuff and get the hell out of here." She exuded a sense of relief. By honestly thinking about my question, she had discovered something about her existential truth: she did not really want to have sex with me, and she was not really hurt by my refusal. The ultimate truth about our relationship was that she wanted me to be her therapist, not her lover.

From that moment onward Ruth's feeling of being utterly dependent on my love began to abate. She felt less and less that she needed to be filled by me. Her dreams indicated that Ruth's sense of self was beginning to consolidate. In one of them, she met a teacher who had helped her a great deal in high school. During this long dream, it turned out that he wanted her to show him many things. What she showed him was primarily connected to Mediterranean landscapes and objects.

Ruth's associations to the dream led to two main conclusions. The first was that she no longer felt dependent on Ashkenazi mentors to develop her selfhood. In the dream, her teacher wanted her to teach *him* things connected to her ethnic provenance. She showed him around, and he learned from her what the Mediterranean was like.

More than three years into the therapeutic process, Ruth reported the following dream:

> I swallowed something unclear. This thing is in my innards now and moves there like the head of a fetus during the advanced stages of pregnancy. You can actually see its round and small contours on my belly, which is both smooth and flat. This thing turns and moves around trying to find a way out from inside my body. I understand that this is a foreign body that I swallowed and that it should not be inside me. I decide to throw up and get it out. I put a finger in my throat and spit it out. What comes out is a small empty glass bottle without a cork. It reminds me of an empty perfume bottle.

Ruth's immediate association to the swallowing was oral sex, and she thought that she had swallowed something of me. First she thought about semen, then about my penis. On one hand. the dream seemed to be an indication that unconsciously Ruth had fulfilled a wish she had nurtured for quite some time. First of all, it meant that she finally had some form of sex with me in the dream. Second, she had incorporated something of me, a theme that had accompanied us for a long time. Yet the dream obviously was not just a wish fulfillment. What she had swallowed felt foreign to her body, and she knew she had to rid herself of it.

During the following sessions Ruth returned to this dream time and again. She told me, "I think that this fantasy of incorporation is a way of not dealing with your actual existence. I am trying to ingest you, so I can give birth to you in a form that is mine and suits my needs. But that also means that I ultimately destroy you. But it turns out that what I have swallowed is a foreign body; I cannot integrate it into myself, and I need to spit it out again."

What struck me was that what came out was an empty perfume bottle. For years now, Ruth had experienced me as containing everything that she wanted to have and to be. And now, strangely enough, the dream showed that all she had ingested was an empty bottle. I felt that this might be an indication that Ruth's desperate sense that she needed to ingest or incorporate me, orally or vaginally, was changing. Didn't the dream also say that she was beginning to realize that our sexual merging was not what she needed in order to become herself? It seemed to me that the dream was a first indication that Ruth was beginning to feel that she had a self of her own that needed to develop and that she did not need to become somebody else.

Shortly after that, Ruth brought another dream.

"You and I are in a ritual of *Chalitza,* in which I liberate you from your obligation. I spit into your shoe and let you go."

Some words of explanation about Biblical law are in order to understand this dream. When a man dies childless, his brother is required to marry his widow (an act called *Yibum).* The first child from this union will be considered the dead brother's. If the living brother refuses to marry his sister-in-law, she releases him from his obligation through the ritual of *Chalitza,* in which she spits into his shoe, saying "Thus shall be done upon the man who refuses to beget offspring for his brother."

The dream condensed a complex emotional reality. *Chalitza* implies that a man has not fulfilled his duty. What was the duty Ruth felt I did not fulfill? Literally, it seemed to imply that I was not giving her offspring. We discussed this, but it did not seem quite right. Ruth's associations led to the conclusion that she felt that I had refused to help her give birth to a new self through a sexual act.

Within this context it is important to take into account, though, that throughout the Jewish Diaspora, the act of *Yibum* has for generations not been performed anymore. The rabbinical tradition was caught between the Biblical injunction to *Yibum* and the sense that this act did not suit contemporary historical circumstances because, among other things, polygamy (allowed by Biblical law) has become unacceptable. The compromise reached was that, whenever the constellation requiring *Yibum* arose, the ritual of *Chalitza* needed to be performed, to liberate the widow to marry someone other than her dead husband's brother.

Against this background, the dream acquired an additional layer of meaning. It seemed to imply a change in Ruth's experience that I was withholding something that was legitimately hers. *Yibum* has been deemed anachronistic for millennia of Jewish history. Did Ruth begin to feel that there was something anachronistic in her demand that I heal her through sex and love?

The transformations in her dreams and transferential experience soon began to translate into her life. After a prolonged period of writer's block, Ruth finally began to feel capable of returning to her graduate thesis. She asked to change its topic and began to focus on the issue of the deep sense of having been wronged that many members of her ethnic group feel. Ruth's conclusions went in a different direction from that of others who harbored those feelings. She argued that, in the experience of many, Western culture had provided them with an opportunity that they might otherwise not have had. Without denying the humiliations and wounds that the Israeli establishment had inflicted on her ethnic group, she emphasized the opportunities Israeli society had provided.

At the time, voices like hers were rare in Israel, for we were then in the heyday of *Shas,* the Sephardic party that had put exclusive emphasis on the need of Sephardic Jewry to return to its traditional way of life. The politics of identity and hatred against the Israeli establishment (embodied most of all in the Supreme Court) were a central theme in the new Sephardic search for a positive identity. Ruth's way of thinking about these issues was rare at the time. She was willing to bear the emotional and political complexity of the tragic history of the relationship between Ashkenazi and Sephardic Jewry in Israel.

In the final phase of the therapeutic process, Ruth found a new mode of integrating her ethnic identity and her desire to be an accepted member of Western culture. She began to see that her own history reflected a wider phenomenon: that Western culture, as embodied in Israeli society, had both rescued and hurt her. Yet she did not turn her work into an accusation against Western society. Her gratitude toward those who had widened her horizon beyond the limitations of her upbringing was great.

She presented aspects of her graduate thesis at several symposia and public events. She called on fellow Sephardic Jews not to embrace the identity of the victim. By showing that Western culture, as mediated through the Ashkenazi elite, had given many of them the possibility of living a richer life, she was arguing for a more complex dialogue both within Sephardic Jewry and between Sephardic and Ashkenazi groups. Ruth was trying, both existentially and intellectually, to overcome the dichotomies between oppressors and victims, on one hand, and "superior" and "inferior" cultures, on the other.

Transference Love: The Personal and the Historical

Ruth's biography raises an intriguing question. Time and again I wondered why the deep wounds and distortions in Ruth's self-experience had not healed in the course of her development. Ruth had made her way into the world. She was, at the time of the therapy, entertaining diplomats from all over the world, attending high-society events, and completing her second degree in anthropology. She had not gotten stuck on the way. Prima facie, her life was a success story. She had yearned to transcend the confines of her upbringing, and she had done so.

She acquired education; grew to be a very attractive adult woman, wooed by many men; and was married to a man who deeply loved her. Alain had wonderfully fulfilled one of Ruth's primary needs: he had immeasurably helped her on her long and painful journey to gain the established place and identity in Western society that she had yearned for since childhood. She accepted, cherished, and reciprocated her husband's love and became an integral part of the social stratum within which he moved. So why had the core of her self-experience remained as wounded as it was?

Ruth's experience is not unique. As I mentioned, I have worked with a considerable number of Sephardic Jews. Some of them are people who have enormous achievements to their credit, ranging from the prominence in the arts through success in academia to the building of business empires. Nevertheless, all of them carried the pain of the experience of growing up with an identity that was considered second rate in Israeli society.

Ruth's dreams of being filled with worms, cockroaches, and filth might easily be attributed to a depressive streak in her genetic makeup. But, as mentioned before, I have seen such dreams in quite a number of Sephardic Jews in Israel, many of whom had no depressive tendency whatsoever. I therefore tend to see these dreams as indicative of something in Israeli social reality.

If I may reiterate briefly, one of the most painful episodes in Israeli history took place when Sephardic Jews who arrived by ship in Israel were sprayed with DDT. The welcome that they received on arriving in the Promised Land was the message, "We assume that all of you are full with lice and other contaminants, and we need to cleanse you of them."

It is my sense that the collective cultural unconscious of Israeli society is permeated with this memory and its implications. As Western culture has done to many other societies, the representatives of Western culture in Israel have projected all its own unacceptable parts into ethnic minorities.

Ruth's relationship to Western culture and the Ashkenazi elite in Israel was tragically complex. On one hand, Western culture for her was a space of liberation. She experienced her own environment as stifling and desperately sought the cultural objects (Bollas 1989) that would allow her to develop aspects of herself that were waiting to evolve. And, indeed, she found many objects to accomplish this evolution—books, ballet, films, and intellectual pursuits, but also in the series of teachers who took it upon themselves to help her develop her potential.

Yet the very same culture and ethnic group that helped her grow had also humiliated her ethnic group and her family. Hence the emotional constellation that she lived in was intolerable: the saviors were also the tormentors who had humiliated her parents to the point of driving her father into alcoholism.

The psychoanalytic understanding of transference and transference love has evolved considerably since Freud's early formulations. From displacement of early object love, a variety of conceptions has evolved. They range from transference as the totality of an object relation (Klein 1952), through transference as the creation of potential space (Winnicott 1971), to the healing functions of selfobject relationships (Kohut 1971) and object use for developing aspects of personal idioms (Bollas 1989), to mention just a few milestones.

Hans Loewald (1960) was among the first to recognize the intrinsically dialectic nature of transferential experience. Transference, in his view, is never just the repetition of an earlier relationship. It is also, always, the search for an essentially new experience. Hence, as Schafer (1983) has shown, transference is always an amalgam of early experience and something quintessentially new. In the same vein, Weiss and Sampson (1986) have argued, transference is always an attempt to master early trauma and pain through the generation of new experience.

Ruth's transference-romance served many developmental purposes. In self-psychological terms, the type of self-disturbance Ruth presented is to be understood as based on parental failures as selfobjects: her father could not really function as a figure for idealization because of the damage the Israeli experience had inflicted on him. Her mother had only a limited ability to help Ruth crystallize her affective experience (Stolorow et al. 1987). Ruth learned to interpret every dangerous situation as potentially lethal. Hence, she needed me both as an object who could help her generate new self-soothing functions (Kohut 1971) and as someone who could be idealized, thus giving her what her parents could not provide at the time.

This basically self-psychological understanding was the main framework that guided me most of the time. Nevertheless it seems to me that a further level needs to be highlighted if we want to gain a deeper understanding of the dynamics of this treatment. Ruth's opening statement was, "I chose you." What was Ruth seeking by choosing me as her therapist? When she had seen me speak publicly, she identified me with the dominant elites that had impressed her so much since childhood. But she had also reacted to something very different–my discomfort with being in the position of lecturer and my sense of strangeness in Israel.

It was this double view of me as insider and outsider that had determined her choice of me as a therapist. Despite all the overt differences between us, she felt that I knew what it was like to feel vulnerable despite the paraphernalia of status, to feel different and a stranger. Behind all the differences, Ruth was seeking a common humanity (Strenger 1998 ch 6). Through the intense emotional encounter with the representative of the Other, she also hoped to find recognition as a like subject (Benjamin 1995). Yes, I was an Ashkenazi male, but I was also a vulnerable stranger.

In her fantasies, our sexual encounter had a very specific character: I would be completely attuned to her, feel her to the deepest core of her being. More than once she said that, in her fantasies, making love to me would be almost like making love to a woman, because I would feel her to a depth that males were not capable of. Behind what may easily seem a projection of phallic completeness, there was the yearning for ultimate sameness.

Through this sameness she felt that I could have cured the damage that the group I was identified with had inflicted on her, her family, and her ethnic group. In spite of all the differences, she was trying to heal herself by experiencing the core of humanness. I was to merge the functions of mentor, lover, therapist and redeemer into something that was like her.

My role was to be both a like subject and a love object, to use Benjamin's (1995) felicitous phrase. Ruth wanted me to be the male Ashkenazi intellectual who would be able to love her as only a woman could. My acceptance of her love for me was to be her ultimate vindication: the oppressor would turn phantasmatic lover, the representative of the Other (also in the Lacanian sense) would become intimate with the minute details of her pain and her wounded self.

It is no coincidence that Ruth chose both a husband and a therapist who were not Israeli born. It is as if there were no way she could meet the group who represented the tormentors of her parents otherwise. Nevertheless she needed to express her need for this group to assume responsibility for the damage it had inflicted on people who were only partially identified with this group.

It is easy to see Western culture in Israel, as reflected by the Ashkenazi elite, as the culprit that inflicted the humiliations of colonialist thinking onto others, be they Sephardic Jews or Arabs, and many such claims can be substantiated (Said 1979). But, for Ruth, Western culture, as she put it, was also a way to move from the 12th to the 20th centuries. Many of the features of Western culture that we are fond of questioning, like individualism and the freedom to build one's identity, were a true epiphany for her.

She experienced her own background as unbearably limiting. For her, the collectivism of her upbringing, the fact that her parents could not relate to children as individuals but only as children, had reduced her to less than she wanted to be. Hence the importance of the teachers and mentors who had recognized her value as an individual and were willing to invest time, love, and energy in her growth.

Ruth's life trajectory was not an attempt to vindicate her ethnic identity: from the age of five, when she wanted to bleach her skin, she sensed that her destiny and desire were to belong to the part of Israeli society that reflected Western culture. All her later life choices pointed in the same direction, and so did the overt intellectual and political stance that she took in her academic work and her social and political activities.

The Reflection of Social and Historical Reality in the Therapeutic Process

Ruth's therapeutic journey reflects an important aspect of the tragedy of Israeli history and society. The founding generation of Israeli society had a dream: to build a country grounded in what they saw as the most progressive vision of a just society, socialism. As recent historical work (Shlaim 1998; Morris 2001) has shown, this founding process created innumerable tragedies: first and foremost, of course, the tragedy of the Palestinian people, which is far from being resolved, but also the tragedy of Sephardic immigrants and their children.

What concerns me here is the deep rift in the identity of Israeli Jewry. It is easy with hindsight to see the cruelty and totalitarianism in Ben-Gurion's dream of a monolithic society based on Zionistic socialism. But we should not forget that, in the 1940s, the socialist dream had not yet disintegrated and it was not yet known that Stalinism had become one of the most inhuman and horrific episodes of human history. Behind the totalitarianism, there was a genuine belief that this was the way to create a just and good society (Eisenstadt 1985).

Furthermore, the idea of the creation of the New Jew may seem both outlandish and cruel from today's vantage point. Yet it is easy to forget that the majority of Jews in Eastern Europe lived in appalling and humiliating circumstances. Disenfranchised politically, mostly poor, they lived in a state of constant hopelessness (Wiesel 1984; Sachar 1986 ch 4).

Even in Western Europe, where Jews had broken free of the chains of political and social disenfranchisement in the 19th century, their self-image was deeply flawed. As Gilman (1986) has shown convincingly, Jews internalized anti-Semitism, and Jewish self-hatred was deeply rooted in the core of Jewish identity. The Jew as a weak, deeply flawed, and pitiful creature was an image that ran through Jewish identity, as expressed by Weininger (1903) .

As Gilman (1993) has demonstrated, the European medical and anthropological literature tried to create a stereotypical racial image of the Jew—an image composed of a dark complexion, dark eyes, dark hair, and distinctly Mediterranean features. In other words, the quintessential Ashkenazi Jew was pictured in the same way we now portray Sephardic Jews! Against the background of recent Israeli history, this fact acquires a tinge of tragic irony.

This is why I propose the following hypothesis: the treatment of Sephardic Jews by the Israeli establishment is based on the projection of the image of the humiliated and dejected Jew in 19th-century European culture. The new Israeli Jew encountered his disavowed past in his kinsmen—and kinswomen—from Arab countries, who looked so much like the stereotype of the dejected European Old Jew. This projection was facilitated by the fact that many Sephardic Jews, upon arrival in Israel, lacked acquaintance with Western institutions and often had very few material belongings. Their lack of sophistication and their poverty evoked the associations of powerlessness that were so strongly associated with the Old Jew. In addition, that most Sephardic Jews were religiously observant created further associations with the Old Jew of the *shtetl* who, instead of defending himself, cried to God to deliver the people of Israel from their suffering.

Ruth's difficult background and wounded self thus reflect both her specific story and a difficult, as yet unresolved piece of Jewish and Israeli history. The drama of her therapeutic encounter with me presents a microcosm of the enormous difficulty involved in creating a Jewish identity viable for present-day Jews in their own state.

Israel will never heal the rift in its society as long as it tries to repress the Jewish Diaspora history that led up to the creation of the Jewish state. That which is repressed inevitably comes to the forefront. The fear of the image of the helpless, second-rate, despised, and self-denigrating Old Jew haunts modern Israeli society despite Israel's having achieved the feat of creating a modern state with a flourishing economy and one of the strongest armies in the world.

Israeli Jewry is faced with a difficult collective task of psychic transformation. Only if it is able to deal with the continuity of Jewish history, rather than splitting it into the pre-Zionist phase of dejection and the era of the creation of the Jewish state and the New Jew, can the rifts in Israeli society be healed.

IDENTITY AND THE SELF: FOUND OR CREATED?

Ruth's story differs from that of the other cases reported in this book in many respects. Her dilemma is less typical of those of Generation X; it resembles the biographical tensions of the children of immigrants in many countries and in many generations before.

Nevertheless, Ruth's biography provides something like an X-ray of the deep structure underlying the motif of the designed self. Her story raises the question, to what extent should we think of personal identity as something that evolves "naturally" through normative stages? To what extent can personal identity be chosen through a conscious act? In other words, to what extent is it appropriate to speak of the self as created rather than found? From very early on in her life, Ruth's destiny drive (Bollas 1989) pushed her toward finding a place in Western society and acquiring an identity within this society. In a childlike way, this deep wish was expressed in her attempt to whiten her skin at age six. Already at that age, she instinctively felt that the place of her upbringing was not suited to the development of her innate distinctiveness.

With remarkable tenacity, she looked for a way out of the environment into which she had been born. She found the cultural and human objects her emerging self needed to elaborate her innate propensities and develop her identity in the Westernized parts of Israeli society. She never accepted the identity assigned to her by birth and strove to form herself according to a different blueprint. which, at that age she could envisage only vaguely.

The project of self-creation is, of necessity, complex and dialectical, because none of us can recreate ourselves from scratch. Whereas most human beings may grow naturally into their identities, many, like Ruth, feel that their preassigned identities fail to address some of their deepest needs and desires. They embark on the project of creating different identities for themselves. This project, in turn, creates rifts in the self and causes wounds that heal only with difficulty.

Could it be, though, that the more painful process of self-creation exemplified by Ruth highlights an essential feature of the human condition in late-modern societies? The darker, more complex visions that were painted by European thinkers like Nietzsche, Heidegger, Sartre, and Foucault provide interesting food for thought about these questions, to which we turn in the next chapter.

Chapter 6

Psychoanalysis in the Age Of the Designed Self

When I presented versions of the various chapters of this book at conferences, lectures, and seminars in different countries, a question kept returning. "What are the implications of your ideas for psychoanalytic theory? Do you have any idea how to turn these insights into a coherent theoretical structure?" My answer was always "no," as, for a variety of reasons, I do not believe in grand theorizing in psychoanalysis (Strenger 1991, 2002).

In this, final, chapter I present a model that makes sense of the current pluralistic atmosphere in psychoanalysis. These are interesting, even though problematic, times for psychoanalysis. At one time it was clear that psychoanalysis was a medical subdiscipline. Then it was clear that it was a psychology. Then again, it was clear that it was a hermeneutic, humanistic undertaking. At this point in psychoanalytic history it is less clear than ever what it is. And this lack of clarity means that we are at a point in time when creative solutions can be offered.

What exactly does the question, what is psychoanalysis? mean, though? In our late-modern age, it certainly does *not* mean to discover the "essence" of psychoanalysis. It could, though, mean that, in trying to understand a human phenomenon, we often metaphorize it. We say, "Business is a sport"; "Sex is war"; "Love is music." Wittgenstein (1953), throughout his later work, investigated the importance of the experience of seeing something as something.

Seeing something as something can be induced by putting it into a series. A simple, and relevant, example is the series into which we can put Sigmund Freud: we can create the series "Galileo, Newton, Lavoisier, Darwin, Maxwell, Freud," and then we view him as a scientist. We can put him into the series "Plato, Aquinas, Spinoza, Nietzsche, Freud," and we will see him as a philosopher. Or, as has been done by authors like Bloom (1994), we can put him into the series "Aeschylus, Dante, Shakespeare, Dostoevsky, Freud" and see him as one of the great figures of world literature who created new modes of narration.

Each of these series allows us to see aspects of Freud's work that we have not seen before, and each of them leads us to value his work differently. The first series puts emphasis on theoretical clarity, predictive power, and consistency with accepted background knowledge. It leads to the well-known problems of ambiguity, difficulties of verification, and inconsistency with present-day biology. The second series puts emphasis on breadth of vision, conceptual clarity. and depth of insight. The last series makes us cherish the very aspects of Freud's work that are problematic in the first series: ambiguity becomes multiplicity of meaning and richness of texture; lack of predictive power turns into interpretive scope.

Psychoanalysis can be metaphorized in different ways, and various modes of seeing psychoanalysis have generated different insights. The medical metaphor has made psychoanalysis seek links with psychiatry and its conceptual tools of diagnoses, treatment techniques. and their outcomes. The psychological metaphor has generated a great deal of interesting research, most of which has been integrated into general psychology. The metaphor of the infant–mother relationship has made us look at the aspects of the psychoanalytic setting that soothe and structure a patient's psyche.

The goal of this chapter is to present a view of psychoanalysis as continuous with the Greco-Roman philosophical schools. Elsewhere I have called this view "Psychoanalysis as Art and Discipline of the Self" (Strenger 1997, 2002). I hope that this metaphorization will help us to make sense of what we do in our daily work, be it with patients, students, and supervisees or in psychoanalytic writing.

From Coherent Theory to Critical Pluralism

Along with such authors as Mitchell (1993) and Phillips (1995), I believe that psychoanalysis needs to give up the vaulting ambitions that made it into one of the dominant explanatory frameworks throughout much of the 20th century. The current pluralistic atmosphere turns psychoanalysis into a playful universe of cultural forms of life. This attitude has turned a necessity into a virtue: the lack of scientific grounding of psychoanalytic thought and practice could leave us with a constant sense that we do not know enough.

Instead, it seems to me, the current climate gravitates toward another option. Psychoanalysis is becoming a loosely connected culture of forming the self. It is an essentially humanistic undertaking organized around a ritualized interaction between two people. Since psychotherapy research (Orbach and Greenberg 2000) indicates that the outcome of therapy does not really hinge on the theory used, it is possible for clinicians to use concepts and metaphors that they prefer on existential, personal, ethical, and aesthetic grounds. If all experience is constructed, then the construction might as well be interesting and satisfying.

This atmosphere has certainly done some good for psychoanalysis: in large sectors of psychoanalysis, it has done away with the type of sectarianism that led clinicians to identify rigidly with one school and to reject the others as shallow, nonanalytic, or otherwise deficient. The result is an ecumenical atmosphere that allows for communication across styles of work. We exist in a pluralist psychoanalytic universe in which it is possible to live and let live.

Many contemporary writers (e.g., Mitchell 1993; Phillips 1995; Aron 1996) have given up the notions of truth and scientific respectability that were once central to psychoanalysis. Instead we relish in a newly gained freedom with which we can build our therapeutic conceptions along our favorite ethical view of life. Feminism, the desire for mutuality and recognition, and the yearning for less monolithic conceptions of selfhood have been at the center of much creative effort in psychoanalytic writing lately (Chodorow 1994; Benjamin 1995). Psychoanalytic pluralism also reflects the deep cultural changes that characterized the generation of Baby Boomers who are, today, the leading psychoanalytic theorists.

Nevertheless, scientific knowledge remains crucial to psychoanalysis. The business of psychoanalysis is the creation of therapeutic narratives. I have argued in the past, and still think, that such narratives should cohere with state-of-the-art scientific knowledge (Strenger 1991 ch 6). I believe that this demand for external coherence is of utmost importance and is far from vacuous in its implications. I believe that it can be shown that some popular psychoanalytic approaches, particularly Kleinian theory, would not survive an examination along the lines of external coherence.

Within these limits of external coherence, however, the creation of narratives that imbue life with meaning is still vastly underdetermined. There are, in other words, many possible ways to narrate human lives that cohere with accepted background knowledge. Elsewhere I (Strenger 1997, 2002) have called this position *critical pluralism.*

I see this pluralism of possible narratives, not as a problem, but, rather, as an ethical and existential necessity. There are, after all, many ways of leading a good life. In the past, when psychoanalysts believed firmly in their favorite theories, they were, in fact, presenting their patients with a particular view of the good life. Doing so did not do any harm if the analyst's ethics harmonized with the patient's personal idiom and ethical beliefs. Harm most certainly is done if the analyst's view does not correspond to the patient's natural propensities. Hence, as I argued in chapter 5, analysts should not work with patients who do not harmonize with their aesthetics of existence. I see the current pluralistic atmosphere (within the bounds of what is consistent with scientific knowledge) as an advantage rather than a weakness.

THE BABY-BOOM REVOLUTION IN PSYCHOANALYSIS: PSYCHOANALYTIC PLURALISM

Let us briefly look at the historical circumstances that brought about what Mitchell (1993, ch. 3) characterized as the paradigm change in psychoanalysis. The Baby-Boom generation grew up into a period of economic growth that, as some historians have argued (e.g., Hobsbawm 1994), may have been unprecedented in human history. During the decades after World War II, living standards increased dramatically for most people in the Western world. For the first time in history the vast majority of people, including the working classes, had access to household appliances that made life easier, and most of them owned cars.

For the generation of those who had lived through the Great Depression and World War II, the achievement of financial security and material comfort was a remarkable accomplishment. Their children, the Baby Boomers, grew up in a reality in which material well-being was becoming a matter of course. Hence, it was not to take long until they saw finding one's place in society, making a living, and raising children an unbearably limiting conception of life.

There is some disagreement about when the grand cultural revolution of Western society came about. Some authors (particularly Roszak 1969) see the 60s as the watershed that changed Western culture. Others (Fukuyama 1999; Frum 2000) argue that the truly momentous changes on a large scale occurred during the 1970s. I am not sure that the two theses truly contradict each other. During the 1960s, the counterculture that was to change the face of the Western world came into being. The Woodstock festival and the student unrest of 1968 might be seen as the two historical icons that embody these changes.

Woodstock exemplified the essence of the hippie generation: free love, dropping out of the system, rock music, and suspicion of the political, social, and economic features of capitalism. The student unrest of 1968 carried these features into the institutions that were supposed to guard, transmit. and develop what is essential to Western culture. When students argued that the teaching bodies had no right to define what was intellectually valid and culturally relevant, they were calling into question the most basic features of what constitutes authority.

During these same years, this authority was being questioned within academia itself. Representatives of critical theory like Herbert Marcuse (1955) and Norman Brown (1955) argued that the foundations of capitalist society were dehumanizing. Marcuse's call for a panerotic society preceded Woodstock by a decade.

The 1960s also saw the emergence of a group of academics who were to shape the more fashionable agenda of the humanities for years to come. The epicenter of this movement that was to become identified as postmodernism was to be found in Paris.

Philosophers like Michel Foucault, Gilles Deleuze, and Jacques Derrida began their deconstruction of some of the most cherished beliefs of Western culture.

Derrida claimed that all of Western philosophy and science was the expression of the highly problematic metaphysical assumption of phallo-logo-centrism. For Derrida, this assumption meant that there was one truth to be uncovered, that language reflected the essence of reality, and that interpretive disciplines could be more than plays of intertextuality.

Foucault's program was no less radical. He questioned the grand historical narrative that saw modernity as a story of progress. In a series of highly influential books, Foucault (1961, 1966, 1976) tried to show that the history of medicine, psychiatry, the human sciences, penal institutions. and attitudes toward sexuality were not a linear development from superstition to knowledge, from irrationality to rationality. Where standard accounts saw liberation and enlightenment, Foucault saw hidden forces of power-knowledge trying to shape human beings into models of normality needed for the management of society.

François Lyotard (1979) was to summarize the general thrust of these agendas as the transition from modernism to postmodernism. He defined the latter as the deep suspicion of all grand narratives of human history. The Enlightenment narrative that took shape during the 18th century was particularly under fire. It assumed that there was progress in human affairs, that Western humanity was moving toward an intrinsic *telos* of history, that is, that were was rationality in the understanding of the natural world and the management of human affairs.

Moreover, the Enlightenment narrative assumed that the history of Western culture was a process of liberation. In Kant's (1783) canonic definition, the Enlightenment was the liberation of the mind from self-imposed tutelage. The intellectuals who were to become the core of postmodern thought raised deep suspicion of this view. They saw the Enlightenment as just another narrative that imposed hidden agendas, interests, and power structures onto individuals and societies.

The process of decolonialization after World War II seemed to indicate that Western culture was indeed not the progressive movement that had led humankind toward liberation. As

Finkielkraut (1995) has shown, the horrors of Western imperialism were used to discredit the cultural backbone of Western culture: humanism and the belief in reason. The confluence of these factors quickly made relativism into the *bon ton* of the day. Anyone who believed in single truths was just caught up in the throngs of phallo-logo-centrism and Eurocentric cultural imperialism.

The politics of identity acquired growing power; previously subjugated ethnic groups and nationalities–African Americans in the United States, Muslims in countries ranging from Algeria to Indonesia, homosexuals in all Western countries–began to demand recognition of their rights, including the right to be different. Postmodernisn, with its deconstruction of set categories of gender, sexuality, rationality, and cultural superiority seemed to be the way to true liberation. People could finally lead authentic lives, discover and live their true sexuality, and be liberated from the straightjacket of entrenched gender roles.

The Baby-Boom generation of psychoanalysts was, of course, sharply shaped by this cultural upheaval. The result was the paradigm change in psychoanalysis referred to earlier (Mitchell 1993). American ego psychology, as it evolved in the 1940s and 1950s, had put a strong premium on adaptation. The ego's ability to bridge the demands of the id, the superego, and the external world commanded the center of attention.

For the Baby-Boom generation, adaptation ceased to be a central value. In fact, it almost became derided. Psychoanalytic writing and practice moved toward what Charles Taylor (1989) called an expressivist view of the human self. In this view, the goal of life is certainly not to adapt to circumstances, to find one's place in society, and to make a decent living. The 60s had turned toward a post-Romantic view of the self: the goal of life was to express one's unique individuality.

This aim was reflected in psychoanalytic writings. Once Baby Boomers like Bollas, Benjamin, and Mitchell (notwithstanding their differences) became leading theorists, the language and the ethos of psychoanalysis began to change. The focus moved from adaptation to helping patients to develop their personal idioms (Bollas) and to enrich their subjectivity (Mitchell).

Feminism became a central driving force: women had finally moved into the work force in large numbers and thus acquired economic independence. The deconstruction of traditional gender roles had enormous influence on the views of baby boom psychoanalysts. Benjamin had witnessed the student revolution in Germany and had studied with some of the theorists of the Frankfurt school, who had provided the students with theoretical tools to criticize existing institutions. She created a rich vocabulary to describe the ways in which women (and men) could be engaged in mutual recognition as like subjects while still being love objects for each others (Benjamin 1995).

Chodorow's (1979) first book was a sustained argument against the traditional view of motherhood and showed that this conception was nothing but a veiled attempt to justify traditional arrangements in which women stayed at home and raised their children essentially alone. Later (1994), Chodorow argued that the very category of heterosexuality was too coarse to describe our sexual experience. In an essentially Foucaldian move, she proceeded to deconstruct the basic dichotomy of normal versus perverse sexuality.

Psychoanalysis moved from a preoccupation with pathology and normality to the search for authentic life styles. Its prevailing political and moral orientation was liberal. Freud's pessimistic view of human nature was replaced by more optimistic views focused on the development of the self like Kohut's (1977) and Winnicott's (1965). The center of attention shifted from inner conflict and outer adaptation to the ways in which parental environment could foster personal growth or fail to do so.

PSYCHOANALYSIS AND CONTEMPORARY GLOBAL CULTURE

It is one of the central arguments of this book that contemporary urban culture has moved one step forward. The notion of the authentic life that psychoanalysis imported from existentialism and humanist psychology has been replaced by a more radical ethic. Life and the self are seen as design projects. It is the task of all of us to create our lives as coherent works that we identify as our own creation. As we have seen through my encounters with patients who live along these lines, this is indeed a tall order, a conception of life that puts high demands on members of urban culture.

If psychoanalysis wants to be able to relate to contemporary global culture, it needs to rethink itself along similar lines. Various psychoanalytic approaches, vocabularies, narratives, and techniques need to be seen as different possible styles of shaping, construing, and narrating lives.

While psychoanalysis is gradually adapting to the idea of pluralism, there is a cultural clash between psychoanalysis and contemporary urban culture that needs to be addressed. Contemporary urban culture has eradicated the differentiation between high culture and low culture (Seabrook 2000). Putting the same state of affairs differently, Zakaria (2003) argues that contemporary culture has been democratized. It has exchanged the question, "Who appreciates a particular work?" for the question, " How *many* are appreciating a particular work?" thus effectively dismantling the idea of a cultural canon.

The canonic conception of culture that defines quality by a set of paradigmatic works that define high culture is currently the focus of sharp debate involving complex cultural and political agendas. Analyzing the issues between the liberal and conservative world views goes beyond the scope of this chapter. What matters to us is that, as a matter of sociological fact, psychoanalysis has, throughout its history, had a highly canonical structure.

What I mean is simple. Most natural sciences value novelty; in physics, biology, and chemistry citations should be as recent as possible. Some journals require that the equipment used in experiments not be older than five years. As opposed to those requirements, psychoanalysis is very much concerned with its own cultural continuity. Most analysts define their identity by allegiance to one or more canonic authors. Modern Freudians, Kleinians, Winnicottians, Bionians, self psychologists, by their very names, emphasize the continuity of their work with a major figure of the psychoanalytic tradition. Hence, psychoanalysis is unique among the social sciences in that almost every publication contains references to theoretical and clinical works some of which were written more than a century ago.

While this tradition is most obvious for writers who have long-term allegiances (e.g., Kleinians, modern Freudians, self psychologists), a basically canonic conception of psychoanalytic culture also characterizes many authors who define their identity through an approach that has evolved in the last two decades. Benjamin's work is a poignant example. Most of Benjamin's writings (1989, 1995) are structured around Freud's works as a starting point. Even though her agenda is innovative and often subversive, her rhetorical strategy is to initiate most of her discussions by analyzing and critiquing Freudian developmental concepts. She introduces many of her own ideas by using Freud's ideas as the Archimedean point through which she defines her own positions.

Benjamin is by no means an exception. The relational approach that evolved through the 1980s and 1990s, while highly contemporary in style and content, derived much of its initial impetus and content from the rediscovery of Sándor Ferenczi's (1932) *Clinical Diary* and its experiments in mutual analysis. Ferenczi, one of Freud's earliest students, had been marginalized, was seen as creative but not quite stable, but was rediscovered as a hero of psychoanalysis. His introduction of the concept of mutuality (more than his actual practice of mutual analysis) allowed the relational school to connect many of its ideas to one of the great historical figures of psychoanalysis.

Elsewhere, I (2002, epilogue) have argued that, in this respect, the dynamics of the history of psychoanalysis is characterized by what literary critic Harold Bloom (1973) has called "the anxiety of influence." Using the blueprint of oedipal dynamics, Bloom has tried to show that the history of English Romantic poetry (and possibly of poetry in general) is driven by what he calls "the strong poet's" anxiety that his or her predecessor has left no space for truly innovative writing anymore. I have tried to show that a similar dynamics characterizes psychoanalytic culture. Freud's paternal shadow looms over all psychoanalytic writing. All "strong" psychoanalytic authors are defined by their desire to carve a space for themselves in which they can introduce truly innovative concepts while maintaining ties to the psychoanalytic tribe.

When it comes to psychoanalytic technique, a similar dynamic holds true. Whereas in most sciences a premium is set on innovative techniques, psychoanalysis sees its foundations in the much discussed so-called classical technique surrounding use of the couch, a frequency of at least four sessions a week, and a focus on transference interpretations. Even those who advocate deviation from this paradigm begin their arguments by discussing classical technique and often define their position by what they reject.

The dynamics of the anxiety of influence has sometimes been fruitful and sometimes pernicious for psychoanalysis. Often the anxiety of losing touch with the analytic past has led to excessive conservatism and preoccupation with matters of ritual rather than substance (e.g., adherence to four times a week on the couch as a definition of "real" psychoanalysis). But in those periods and places in which the richness of the history of psychoanalysis has been an inspiration for critical discussion, and for those authors who have been similarly inspired, intergenerational continuity and tension have been productive.

The culture of psychoanalysis is richly historical. It is an endeavor that is by its nature preoccupied by the way the past informs the present. This connection holds true for the understanding of individual patients as well as for the understanding of psychoanalysis itself. In this sense, psychoanalysis is a humanistic discipline *par excellence.*

There is therefore an inevitable clash between psychoanalytic culture and several central characteristics of contemporary ahistorical culture. The latter has little room for intergenerational continuity, conflict, and tension, whereas psychoanalysis makes these topics the center of both its theoretical content and its cultural structure.

I have documented this clash in many variations. In my encounter with Iris, I needed to reexamine many psychoanalytic developmental assumptions in order to maintain dialogue with her. Working with Iris required that I refrain from being judgmental of her search for the right style, a search that sometimes pushed her to extremes. I believe that, if I had pathologized her search rather than accepting it as a step toward her finding her voice and a sense of authorship, we would not have been able to do fruitful work.

In my work with Ben, this problem was most pronounced: with him I had to deviate radically from an analytic style of working in order to make meaningful contact with him. Yet, even though my work did not *look* analytic, I do not feel that I lost contact with analytic thought, and within myself I conceptualized the clinical process in analytic terms. We took off only when I abandoned the analytic stance eloquently described by Schafer (1983). My encounter with Yaron necessitated discussions of the cultural ideals that dominated his life, even though those discussions were far removed from classical technique.

These instances are a reflection of the deep tension between the spirit of psychoanalysis and many aspects of contemporary urban culture. I have shown how I have tried, on an individual basis, to mediate between two conflicting needs. On one hand, my clinical identity is very much based on a critical dialogue with the psychoanalytic tradition, and hence it is difficult for me to do therapeutic work without connecting to it. On the other hand, my clinical ethos (along with that of many contemporary clinicians and authors) requires that I try to understand and meet patients on their own ground.

Psychoanalysis as a Family of Ethico-Philosophical Schools

An alternative metaphor for psychoanalysis is, I believe, fruitful and instructive for the historical present, even though it connects psychoanalysis to the distant past of European culture (see Strenger 2002 *passim,* and particularly epilogue). Ellenberger (1970 p. 501) stated an intriguing thesis: Freud's greatest achievement, in his view, was not the discovery of the unconscious, not the psychoanalytic theory of development or mental functioning under conditions of conflict, or the creation of the analytic attitude. Freud's greatest achievement, he said, was Freud's revival of the tradition of the Greco-Roman philosophical schools.

That thesis is strange. The Greco-Roman philosophical schools are generally conceived of as speculative traditions that developed and taught metaphysical and ethical systems. Yet, as intellectual historian Hadot (1995) has shown, this image of the Greco-Roman schools is profoundly misleading. These schools were institutions intended to train students in a whole way of life. The metaphysical systems were the theoretical background that justified this way of life, and teaching their contents was but one part of the training.

The centerpiece of these schools was "mental training," the acquisition of mental and spiritual capacities that were to be translated into every aspect of life. For example, the stoic doctrine emphasized that the trained mind, after understanding the *logos* of the world, needed to differentiate between necessary and unnecessary desires. The more desires a human being has, the more dependent he is on the external world. Since the stoic ideal of selfhood emphasized inner freedom and dignity, philosophical training was geared to minimize dependence on the external world.

Another example: The neo-Platonist tradition claims that the highest degree of human development is reached when a person experientially connects to the emanation of the One that is the source of all being and all goodness. Hence, in addition to metaphysical instruction, philosophical training consists of spiritual exercises that generate mystical states of oneness with higher metaphysical realms.

Ellenberger's (1970) thesis now becomes more intelligible. The Greco-Roman schools were no less institutions that trained mind and character than they were theoretical systems of thought. Hence they are part of the cultural traditions that are intended to form the person as a whole.

Conceptions of ideal selfhood and virtue cannot remain purely theoretical if they are to guide individuals in the development of their personalities. Those concepts must receive concrete embodiment in the cultural institutions that create practices of disciplining the self (Foucault 1983). Well-known examples of such institutions are schools of meditation, which are geared to training people to achieve control over their states of mind and autonomous bodily functions; military academies, which, besides the theoretical knowledge and skills they teach, are supposed to develop personality characteristics desirable for military officers; and monastic orders, which teach theological knowledge and pastoral skills and also train novices to develop such personality traits as humility, temperance, love of God, and the like.

The practices of these institutions depend on the ideal personalities they want to develop: Zen masters want to develop emptiness, the capacity for immediate experience, calmness. and effortlessness of concentration in order to reach enlightenment. Hence, meditative practices are geared to the purification of thought, training the imagination to visualize certain images and metaphors, and developing the ability to focus on immediate bodily experience (Buswell 1992). Military academies work to inculcate subordination through drill, leadership through exercise of judgment in maneuvers, stamina through prolonged physical exercise and standing up to hardship, and reliability through the development of relevant skills and the like. Monastic orders try to instill belief by prayer, temperance through abstinence and fasting, humility through subordination to one's superiors, love of God through meditation, and study (Strenger 2002).

The metaphorization of psychoanalysis as akin to philosophical schools highlights what I consider to be very important aspects of psychoanalysis. It creates the context of the long series of cultural traditions that tried to provide its members with a whole way of life. A person entering analytic training is not just instructed in theories, but undergoes a process of training intended to reach the innermost core of the psyche. Lately, psychoanalysis has begun to follow up on this idea, as is documented by several publications (Spezzano and Gargiulio 1997; Strenger 1997, 2002).

Freud (1933) always claimed that he did not have a *Weltanschauung* and that he did not have an ethical view. Elsewhere, I have argued that nothing could be further from the truth (Strenger 1991 ch 6). Freud had an integrative vision of human life and a clear precept for a good way of living it. Freud is one of the most important modern representatives of the stoic ethical tradition. Seeking dignity and serenity, Freud argued for the renunciation and acceptance of the discontent engendered by civilization. Psychoanalysis, in Freud's version, is a battle designed to conquer areas of the mind for the reality principle. This stoic cast of mind is a particular way of interpreting the human condition, and it entails a particular discipline of the self to deal with its pitfalls, difficulties, pains, and conflicts.

Some recent examples of alternative psychoanalytic interpretations of the human condition call for examination. Two of them bear a family resemblance to a major Hellenistic philosophical school. Eigen (2002) sees himself as an heir to the neo-Platonic tradition with its emphasis on spiritual ecstasy. Phillips (1995) holds psychoanalysis to be (or become) an "interesting hedonism" (p. xvii). Hedonism is the ethics of another of the central Hellenistic philosophical schools, Epicureanism. I will then turn to a characterization of what I take to be the ethos of the relational movement, even though it is specifically late-modern, and any connection to a specific Greco-Roman school would be anachronistic. Finally I argue that European existentialism, even though not *en vogue*, provides an interesting partner for dialogue in the age of the designed self.

My goal is not to write intellectual history. It is, rather, to highlight the family resemblance of psychoanalysis and the tradition of disciplines of the self like the Greco-Roman schools. In particular, I believe that not enough attention has been paid to the fact that every style of psychoanalysis (and psychotherapy in general) entails what I have elsewhere (Strenger 2002) called "aesthetics of the self," by which I mean a vision of the good life, a preferential ordering of the various goods, and an emotional tone dominant in viewing life (e.g., tragedy, comedy, the epic quest; Schafer 1976; Strenger 1989). But, most of all, an aesthetic of existence presents an image of what it would be like to live a life along the lines proposed, and proposes ways to train and shape the self that would put such an aesthetic of existence into action.

Michael Eigen's Psychoanalytic Mysticism: Finding Joy in the Valley of Tears

> *"I went further and further into [the pain], and then, all of a sudden . . . the pain opened up and became radiant light."*
>
> –Eigen, quoted in Molino

Eigen (1998) sees himself as a psychoanalytic mystic. His master-narrative indeed reflects the long line of mystical writers who describe the journey from agony to ecstasy. Within the context of Western culture the neo-Platonic tradition has been the carrier of this narrative for two millennia from Plotinus through Italian Renaissance thinkers like Pico della Mirandola and Giordano Bruno (Kristeller 1979; Hadot 1995) to Jungian thought and practice (Hillman 1975).

Most mystics tell personal stories of their path to enlightenment. Eigen makes use of personal stories in a similar vein. The story he tells is that of a man who had to struggle through a lot of pain. From adolescence onward he read depth psychological books and found meaning and solace in them. He chose a career in clinical psychology but did not feel that he really belonged with the insiders of the profession he had chosen. The pain of not belonging is both a torture and the starting point of a spiritual journey. Like most mystics, Eigen has deep emotional experiences that change him forever. Let me quote the passage that contains the full text of the quotation I cited at the beginning of this section.

> I can think back at when I was in my 20s, on a bus, being in extreme agony. I just suddenly lost consciousness and dipped into this sense of agony, and stayed with an agony that seemed to be located in my chest. It was a terrible psychological pain, not a physical pain so much as a horrendous emotional pain, that I imagined and felt in my chest area. I went further and further into it, and I doubled over on the bus, and then all of a sudden, quite surprised– not having any mental frame of reference for what was happening–the pain opened up and became radiant light. Where before there was just agony and horrendous pain, without my knowing what had happened, suddenly there was bliss. It turned into a terrific light that left me wishing it would never end. Of course, the pain didn't go away, but the bliss has never left me either [quoted in Molino 1997 pp. 96–97].

Eigen's master narrative is condensed in this episode. His work, more than 30 years later, explores the area between catastrophe and faith and the journeys that can lead from psychic deadness to joy. The twist of the story is to be found in its setting. Eigen does not tell us about enlightenment while he is in a Tibetan monastery or looking at the Grand Canyon. It is all happening on a bus, presumably in New York City. We do not know why young Michael is in such excruciating pain; there is no insinuation of a metaphysical crisis. It may be anything from the feeling of not belonging to a disappointment in love. But what Eigen learns on this bus ride is that there is a deep link between catastrophic pain and spiritual bliss.

Throughout the years, we are told, Eigen has read voraciously, and much of his development is an intense intellectual and existential confrontation with some of the main theories and figures of the psychoanalytic tradition. But intense personal encounters have made a great difference. Besides his own analyses, he talks of his encounters with two of his own "masters," Winnicott and Bion.

His account of these encounters is both fascinating and instructive. Eigen emphasizes how strange both Winnicott and Bion were as human beings. He speaks of Winnicott's awkwardness and Bion's detachment. What he took from these encounters was a sense of legitimacy in becoming who he was. Speaking of Winnicott's awkwardness, he came to the conclusion that Winnicott emanated, "If I can be Winnicott, you can be Michael Eigen." Eigen speaks of the sense of being a mutant, of not belonging, and of the new possibility of turning painful experience into a developed sense of his own individuality.

This ability and willingness to go his own way ultimately leads to a consolidation both on the personal and on the public level. Eigen is fringe theater that has conquered Broadway. He has taken his own meandering ways through readings, personal encounters, and analytic experiences both as patient and as analyst outside the centers of the psychoanalytic establishment. In the last 20 years he has generated an *oeuvre* that through the sheer density of its voice has gained a place of growing centrality and recognition. In the manner of all spiritual traditions, Eigen's *oeuvre* is an attempt to learn from his personal story and to generate a narrative that is applicable to therapeutic journeys for others as well.

THE DIMENSION OF THE SACRED IN LATE MODERNITY

> *"Therapy may involve skill, but it is also a form of prayer."*
> –Eigen

How does Eigen transform his personal enlightenment experience on a bus into a therapeutically viable master narrative? In his master narrative, he faces bottomless psychic pain and transforms it into hope once he has reached the bottom level. His main guide and companion on this transformation is Wilfred Bion, for whom gaining the ability to suffer one's pain was the main objective of the psychoanalytic process and who was sympathetic to Eigen's own mystical predilections. Throughout the years Eigen has written a series of papers in which he retraces Bion's thoughts on catastrophe, the black hole, and the pain of regaining psychic truth.

But, unlike Bion, Eigen is less concerned with the destructive tendencies of the psychotic core. Eigen's own mysticism is less transcendentally inclined than Bion's, and he lightens the dark colors of Bion's austere vision of the psychoanalytic process as the discipline of bearing mental pain. Winnicott, in his own way a mystic, even though a very inner worldly one, provides Eigen with a narrative that emphasizes the possibility of joy in the encounter with the other. Other major figures in Eigen's dialogue include Marion Milner and Jacques Lacan (even though in an idiosyncratic version).

Eigen's psychoanalytic mysticism is tempered by a strenuous intellectual effort to conceptualize his personal experience in an intense dialogue with the psychoanalytic tradition. Eigen does not slide into a Gnostic position that gives mystical experience some absolute truth value. Neither is his mysticism of the Bionian kind, which ends up with the ineffability of absolute psychic reality.

The opposite is true: over the years Eigen has developed and honed a truly extraordinary ability to transform affective experience into written language. He writes about therapeutic work in great detail, and with remarkable openness about his own experience, and thus eschews another danger of mysticism, namely, the guruization of the mystic. He never succumbs to the temptation actually to become a mystic seer telling his flock about his wisdom.

Eigen's psychoanalytic mysticism is, I believe, an interesting answer to one of the pervasive problems of many patients nowadays: the disappearance of the sense of a selfhood and of the dimension of the sacred.

Eigen's clinical work is a search for the sacred within. He does so not by adding to neoconservative lamentations and does not see his task as normalizing patients into traditional roles. To the contrary, Eigen is more willing than most analysts to go along with his patients' idiosyncrasies and their very particular mind sets. In this respect, Eigen follows in the footsteps of those Chassidic Mystic masters like Mendel of Kotzk and Nachman of Bratslav, who were more attracted to outsiders than to the establishment.

Eigen has a strong sense of the sacred: if one does not have a focus of numinous experience, one will of necessity relinquish the possibility of being truly alive. His (1966) *Psychic Deadness* deals with the experience of not finding the sacred, the center that makes for aliveness. He proposes that a patient who is lost in a multitude of possibilities that he cannot negotiate find a center within. Eigen does so not by indoctrinating the patient or offering teachings. Rather, he offers an intense, very personal encounter that gives the patient the experience of true otherness. Eigen interprets Winnicott's (1969) idea of the use of the object as experiencing the joy that the other is *truly* other, out of the reach of fantasied destruction. The dimension of the sacred for Eigen is sometimes one of terror, but mostly one of intense aliveness. In the real encounter with the other, the patient will find a core of true aliveness within.

Time, Pain, and the Emergence of Meaning

> *"You might want to help a person view therapy as a kind of psychic gymnasium."*
> –Eigen, quoted in Molino

All great spiritual traditions from Plato's academy to Zen Buddhism have emphasized that spiritual experience demands mental *discipline.* Enlightenment and bliss have to be acquired through mental balance and poise. In this respect, Eigen also retains his link to these traditions. The idea of therapy as a psychic gymnasium captures exactly that idea: the soul must build the ability to weather emotional storms if a meaningful life is to be lived.

There seems to be a fact about the human psyche that is at odds with this saturation by readily available stimuli. The psyche needs *time* to imbue objects, people, images, and words with meaning. At the deepest level, Eigen's clinical work seems to me to be about time, about the possibility of seeing what happens when we let time evolve. This possibility has been recognized by all spiritual traditions. The motif of the *journey* is crucial to all of them. The soul needs time to generate meaning. To avoid a sense of mystification, the same fact can be expressed in the language of science, as we will no doubt find the neurobiological foundation for that fact soon. To imbue an object with meaning, countless modules of neurons need to interconnect, and the brain, as opposed to digital computers, creates interconnection through experiential input. We cannot be fed meaning through CD ROMs.

Most spiritual traditions address a second fact: the creation of deep meaning is connected to the experience of pain. One of the things that will happen, if we take the time to delve into our psyche, is that we will be in pain. We encounter the pain of emptiness, of lack, of failure, of loss. Spiritual discipline requires us to bear that pain if we are to find new meanings. It does not seem possible to generate meaning in the quick-fix mode of instant happiness. This is why psychoanalytic therapy cannot work quickly, but takes time; and it is also why the analytic process inevitably entails suffering psychic pain.

Eigen's work is about the possibility that, if you stay with the pain long enough, joy may emerge. It is about the faith that even pain is preferable to psychic deadness and that suffering pain can ultimately lead to true aliveness and joy.

The psychic gymnasium of the psychoanalytic situation requires discipline (as does physical training and the pain it entails). The spirit of Eigen's work is opposed in interesting ways to the softer edges *en vogue* in many therapeutic quarters. He does not seek to be attuned to the patient's needs at every moment or to create an atmosphere of warmth. Eigen is very human and humane in his therapeutic presence, but not by accommodating to the patient's needs and desires. By trying to help his patients face their existential and psychic catastrophe, Eigen can be tough: he does not compromise psychic lucidity and truth.

Psychoanalytic Epicureanism: Adam Phillips

Epicureanism is generally associated with the unbridled search for pleasure. The term hedonism is also understood as a basically gluttonous conception of life. Historically the Epicurean school stood for something very different though. Of what must have been a vast corpus of writing by Epicurus, only some fragments have survived, and most of what is known about Epicurus is derived from Diogenes Laertius's (1925) *Lives of Eminent Philosophers,* and the most systematic presentation of Epicurean philosophy is to be found in Lucretius's philosophical poem *De Rerum Natura* (Gaskin 1995).

First of all, Epicurean philosophy opposes what it deems unnecessary and irrational fear. Lucretius presents Epicurean atomism as the way to avoid fear of the gods. There is no externally imposed fate. Life is a contingent series of events governed by the blind play of atoms. Hence there is no reason to be afraid of external sanctions and punishment for our actions. All we can do is structure our lives as wisely as possible to minimize pain and maximize pleasure. We need to cultivate friendship, not be blinded by external failure and success, and find ways to live cheerfully in a universe that is essentially indifferent to us (Gaskin 1995).

One of the most original and prolific psychoanalytic writers of the last several years, Phillips (1995), proposes that "if psychoanalysis cannot tell people how to live, it *should* still be able to make people feel better, but often in unexpected ways. . . . It should, in other words, be that most unlikely thing: an interesting hedonism" (p. xvi). With this proposal, Phillips puts himself squarely into the Epicurean tradition—even though he does not choose to make explicit reference to it.

Phillips has developed a highly idiosyncratic voice. He writes in the tradition of Montaigne (1958), the most influential renaissance Epicurean, whose *Essays* are explorations of the self. Montaigne's skeptical meditations are spiritual exercises meant to liberate the mind from excessive preoccupations, fears, and superstitions.

Phillips's literary genre is indeed the essay; in fact Frank Kermode (1994) has gone so far as to say that "Phillips has virtually invented the essay as a suitable form for penetrating psychoanalytic enquiry." Unlike an academic monograph, none of his writings are learned disquisitions that investigate topics empirically or theoretically. Phillips eschews most major psychoanalytic journals and instead publishes in reviews that border on the literary. His writings can be seen as secular sermons, as attempts to induce in the reader the state of mind that Phillips recommends as beneficial for a happier life.

Against Psychoanalytic Pomposity

Phillips is Epicurean first and foremost by trying to liberate psychoanalysts from fears instilled by the psychoanalytic tradition. With sometimes playful and sometimes biting irony, he takes the psychoanalytic establishment to task for a variety of sins. The sin Phillips is least tolerant of is pomposity. He relentlessly attacks the wrong ways psychoanalysis takes itself: he muses about the crippling preoccupation of psychoanalysts with the true essence of psychoanalysis (1995 p. xvi), about the ways in which psychoanalysis is constantly dealing with itself instead of wondering about human beings.

In his view, psychoanalysis has turned from an exercise in liberation into a source of fears:

> Most psychoanalytic theory now is a contemporary version of the etiquette book; improving our internal manners, advising us on our best sexual behaviour (usually called maturity, or mental health, or a decentered self). It is, indeed, dismaying how quickly psychoanalysis has become the science of the sensible passions, as though the aim of psychoanalysis was to make people more intelligible to themselves rather than to realize how strange they are. When psychoanalysis make too much sense, or makes sense of too much, it turns into exactly the symptom it is trying to cure: defensive knowingness [Phillips 1995 p. 87].

Psychoanalytic institutions are so concerned with the purity of psychoanalysis, with its essence and the continuity of its traditions, that they have become sources of authoritarian indoctrination rather than of practices of emancipatory liberation. Phillips is relentless in pointing out how dangerous this preoccupation with itself is to psychoanalysis and how useless it is to its patients.

For Phillips, the desirable outcome of an analytic encounter is not a well-analyzed person. He is highly wary of any such notion. Standard analytic thinking is too likely to produce people who have replaced one set of mental etiquette with another one. Phillips measures life by what I would call a coefficient of eroticism. His question would not be "How mature/balanced/objectrelated/integrated is this person?" I assume that the Phillipsian diagnostic criterion would be something like, "How interesting is it to live this person's life?"

If the goal of psychoanalytic treatment is to make people more interesting to themselves, it follows that "psychoanalysis, as theory and practice, should not pretend to be important instead of keeping itself interesting (importance is a cure for nothing)" (p. xvi).

Phillips has stated quite explicitly (in Molino 1997) that he invites his readers to use his texts as fishing ponds, where they may find fish that they find tasty. In other words, Phillips tries to write texts that attempt, by themselves, to be pleasurable.

This goal is certainly consistent with the "strange hedonism" that he wants psychoanalysis to be. But it is also an attempt to practice what he preaches. If psychoanalysis should try to be interesting (p. xvi), one of the ways to implement this credo is to write psychoanalytic texts that are pleasurable to read.

The serious intent behind Phillips's playfulness is to dismantle psychoanalytic authoritarianism. Phillips successfully avoids the trap of many critics of authoritarianism: to attack one form of authoritarianism while at the same time creating a new form of the same illness. The reader who looks for authoritative statements about anything in Phillips's (at this point voluminous) work is constantly disappointed. Unlike many writers who argue against earlier theories by establishing a new one, Phillips goes out of his way to avoid anything that could be mistaken for theorizing, systematic or otherwise.

His writing always takes care to remain playful, associative, *scriptible* rather than *lisible* (readable), to use Roland Barthes's distinction. Phillips's obvious pleasure in writing, his humor, and his irony can induce in the reader the most unlikely of reactions to a psychoanalytic text. I have actually laughed while reading some of his passages. Then, in shock, I noticed that I had never before laughed when reading about psychoanalysis! And, Phillips would argue, if psychoanalysis never makes you laugh, there must be something seriously wrong with it (psychoanalysts do, of course, write about humor, but the writing is never funny!).

Phillips is not the first psychoanalytic writer who claims to be antiauthoritarian. His great French predecessor is Lacan, who incessantly argued against mistaking the psychoanalyst for the "subject supposed to know." Yet Phillips is a lot more consistent in this position than was Lacan, whose writings and seminars abound with the expression "our teachings." Lacan, while claiming to be subversive, consistently turned himself into a guru, as Roudinesco (1996) has shown in impressive detail.

Phillips cannot be accused of the same inconsistency. Where Lacan made a big issue of being excommunicated by the IPA, Phillips just issues a dry statement that, as far as he is concerned, anyone who uses the primary concepts of psychoanalysis is a psychoanalyst.

Interestingly, his strategy works. Instead of trying to build a school, he builds a readership. Instead of trying to gather followers, he evokes interest. His strategy is totally consistent with his view that psychoanalysis should be interesting rather than important.

The Celebration of Desire

Phillips's playfulness has a therapeutic intent. If, as he says, people seek out psychoanalysis because they are too much for themselves (1995 p. xii), the one thing that will not help them is an authority that represents an orderly way of living, feeling, and, of course, desiring. Instead, psychoanalysis, in Phillips's Epicurean view should enhance people's ability to desire.

Phillips's enemy is what he calls *Procrusteanism,* quoting Emanuel Ghent appreciatively (Phillips 2002 p. 129). As it is, our upbringing scares us to death. We are taught to see ourselves as dangerous. Civilization, as Freud (1930) pessimistically noted, inevitably creates discontent because it needs to curb desire. The Procrustean bed of civilized behavior is likely to leave us without true desires, because we all desperately try to model our desires on the standards of what is acceptable. Alas, by trying to normalize desire we end up with sanitized versions that have very little to do with pleasure, which, after all, is an intrinsic component of desire.

Desire, supposedly, is a central focus of psychoanalysis. Yet there is very little celebration of desire in psychoanalytic writing. If anything, much psychoanalytic theorizing is busy classifying and explaining desire to the point of emptying it of pleasure. After all, once you have analyzed and explained (or explained away) all that is desirable about an object or an activity, you may be left with a tight explanatory framework but very little that is desirable.

Phillips takes a very different approach. Psychoanalysis, in his Epicurean version, helps people to find out how strange they are, not so they will find an explanation for that strangeness, but to make them enjoy it. Completely unafraid of potential accusations that he is strange, Phillips (1995) points out that the life of desire is opposed to lucidity: "There is nothing like sexuality, of course, for making a mockery of our self-knowledge. In our erotic lives, at least, our preferences do not always accord with our standards. We are excited by the oddest things, and sometimes people" (p. 87).

Standard psychoanalytic thinking would now proceed to an explanation of these oddities: we are excited by strange stuff because we are orally fixated, are stuck in the schizoparanoid position, or put a screen between ourselves and our objects of desire. The list of explanations could be lengthened. Phillips does not add another explanation. He also does not, authoritatively, tell us something about the nature of desire. He just lets this sentence hang in midair , and everyone is invited to see what it evokes in our minds. If it evokes interest and pleasure, Phillips, the Epicurean, might well be pleased.

The Celebration of Contingency: Against the Obsession with Explanation

Another point at which Phillips (1993) (again without explicit reference, and possibly unknowingly) connects to the Epicurean tradition is in his celebration of contingency. He is profoundly opposed to the obsession of many analytic writers and practitioners with explanations of behavior, psychic dynamics, and mental contents according to their pet models. Instead, Phillips proposes a celebratory stance toward the very unexplainability of who we are. We should celebrate our strangeness and cherish the quirkiness of our life trajectories.

Phillips looks neither for ultimate explanations of how our symptoms evolved or for how exactly we became what we are. Turning terror into meaning for him is not a matter of finding the right interpretation. This is why Phillips (1995) thinks of psychoanalysis as having a conversation, not as a sophisticated technique in which the analyst uncovers the patient's unconscious nor as a systematic dismantling of the analysand's defenses. By having a certain type of conversation, the patient can gradually move from a stance in which she is too much for herself, to the enjoyment and interest in being who she is.

What, then, about the psychoanalytic tradition of explaining who we are? Phillips has no sympathy for this obsession with explanation. He sees human lives as contingent, both for the species (1999) and for the individual (1994). Contingency, for many, is a source of terror. We would like to feel that there is something unavoidable in our being who we are. Hence the importance many attach to some sort of true self, a blueprint embedded in our being that directs our development to where it should be.

Bollas has been the most eloquent spokesman of this direction of thought and has developed a rich vocabulary to describe the processes through which a personal idiom can evolve. Phillips (1988), while not unsympathetic to Bollas (he acknowledges Bollas as one of his teachers), has moved in a different direction. What, he asks, would happen if we were to stop seeking the deep sources of our selfhood? What would happen if we were to conclude that there is no explanation for who we are, but we could just marvel at the very fact that we are who we are?

Phillips, in the Epicurean tradition, sees contingency as a cause for celebration rather than mourning. If we are basically unintelligible to ourselves, we might as well take wholehearted interest in ourselves. If there is no ultimately true story about ourselves, we might as well try to tell our stories in ways that celebrate existence.

This is why whenever Phillips writes about the history of psychoanalysis, he looks for the interesting anecdote rather than for deep continuities. His (1995 ch 2) essay on the relationship between Freud and Ferenczi does not attempt to analyze the deep rift, or the theoretical differences, between the two men. Rather, he points out how their characters and relationship reflect different conceptions of the relationship between authority and intimacy. When he writes about Freud, he seeks out the interesting bits rather than a profound illumination of Freud's life. "A biography might be like a parodic monument of our wishful relationship to the dead, and to the living" (Phillips 1999 p. 107).

Thus we have come to Phillips's (1999) most Epicurean book, *Darwin's Worms*. Epicureans have always been at pains to argue that we should not be afraid of death, and Phillips's book is, in its own way, an essay disassembling this fear. By meditating on Darwin's interest in earthworms and Freud's relationship to death, Phillips attempts to make the subject of death an occasion for musing rather than for terror. Of course, Phillips does not take the route of logical argument, as his Epicurean predecessor Lucretius did. Instead, he writes enjoyably and intriguingly about the ways in which Darwin turned the human species into a contingent development and the ways in which Freud faced his own death.

If contingency is a cause for celebration, psychoanalysis, in Phillips's view, should learn how to celebrate it. This is why his books have titles like *On Kissing, Tickling and Being Bored* (1993) and *On Flirtation: Essays on the Uncommitted Life* (1994). The latter title might come as an insult to those who think that psychoanalysis should be a deeply committed study of human nature. But Phillips thinks that it is actually consoling to liberate ourselves from ideas that tie us down to commitments to illusions. And the explainability of human life for him is just such an illusion.

The Ethical Dimension of Psychoanalysis

Eigen and Phillips provide two interesting alternatives to the stoic model of psychoanalysis that has been dominant since Freud. Eigen's neo-Platonist, Mystic version of psychoanalysis moves the axis of psychoanalytic thought from the tension between the pleasure principle and the reality principle to the polarity of agony and ecstasy. Renunciation and self-knowledge is not Eigen's final goal. At the end of suffering, there must be ecstasy and joy. It is worth meeting one's psychic catastrophe only if at the end of the process there are at least moments of bliss, when colors shine brighter, the Other becomes a source of joy, and existence is experienced in more depth.

Eigen creates versions of Winnicott and Lacan that connect his own mystical intuition with the psychoanalytic tradition. As he himself emphasizes, particularly his use of Lacan is idiosyncratic, but it certainly reaches its goal–through the concept of *jouissance,* Eigen connects his own sense of the possibility of bliss to an established psychoanalytic author.

In so doing, Eigen creates a paradigm of psychoanalytic creativity. In this brief reconstruction of what I take to be a central thread in Eigen's narrative of personal development we have seen how he moves between his own intense, personal experience and the psychoanalytic tradition. His use of personal experience allows him to go beyond the boundaries of most versions of psychoanalysis. His use of classic analytic texts in conceptualizing this experience makes the experience available to others as an intersubjectively valid version of psychoanalytic thought and practice.

Eigen's psychoanalytic mysticism certainly adds an interesting version of the good life that might be used as a counterbalance even by those who may not necessarily endorse it entirely. Eigen's preference for the extremes of affective experience reminds us that the more traditional accounts of the good life, reasonable and useful as they are, also carry a price.

Phillips cherishes Eigen's work—he edited a collection of Eigen's papers (Phillips 1993). Yet I believe that in many ways he is at the opposite end of the spectrum of possible aesthetics of existence. Where Eigen seeks metaphysical drama, Phillips seeks ironic deconstruction of unnecessary drama. Where Eigen seeks pathos and ecstasy, Phillips is opposed to pathos and seeks lightness of touch.

Phillips's psychoanalytic Epicureanism (to which, you may have noticed, I am drawn more than to Eigen's mystic neo-Platonism) adds a fascinating, and I believe important, voice to the psychoanalytic picture of human reality. By relentlessly opposing the tendency of psychoanalysis to take itself terribly seriously, Phillips opens a possibility that has eluded psychoanalysis for most of its history: he makes us appreciate the enormous potential of lightness of touch, humor, and irony in looking at the intractability of human lives.

The success of Phillips's writings both within and beyond psychoanalytic circles shows how relevant his voice is in a world that has lost many of the certainties of the past, and he opens the possibility of doing psychoanalytic work that is not obsessed with purity of technique and adherence to tradition. Instead he finds new ways of making us (in a deep sense) interesting to ourselves as human beings.

MUTUALITY, INTERSUBJECTIVITY, AND RECOGNITION: A NEW PSYCHOANALYTIC ETHOS

In the mid-1980s a new psychoanalytic ethos began to evolve. At the beginning, it seemed that some specific theoretical and clinical issues were being addressed by a variety of authors. In 1983 Greenberg and Mitchell published their seminal *Object Relations and Psychoanalytic Theory.* This was primarily an expository *tour de force* by two young authors who described a paradigm shift from theories focused on drives and psychic structure to a personality theory centered on object relations.

At the same time, Irwin Hoffman began to publish a series of papers (collected in Hoffman 1999), in which he raised several questions. To what extent did patients' experience of their analysts reflect the analyst's actual subjectivity? Was the model of transference as purely the reflection of the analysand's unconscious too simplistic? Could it be that the analysand related to actual features of the analyst? Furthermore, could it be that this recognition of the analyst's personality was not just a disturbance of the "pure," "uncontaminated" analytic process, but an essential feature of it?

In 1989 two seminal books appeared: Stephen Mitchell's *Relational Concepts in Psychoanalysis* and Jessica Benjamin's *Bonds of Love.* Mitchell examined a variety of issues central to psychoanalytic thinking: autonomy versus dependence, authenticity versus compliance, health versus mental disturbance. His argument was that all these dichotomies were being handled too rigidly by earlier psychoanalysis. They had been given a clear direction in which it was always clear how in "normal" development human beings moved from one pole to the other. Mitchell argued that, instead, all these concepts needed to be put into a wider context, that they reflected different facets of human experience, and that many tenets of long-held psychoanalytic creeds needed to be reexamined.

Thus Mitchell led a conceptual revolution. Heralding a new style of psychoanalytic thinking that reexamined the most fundamental tenets of psychoanalysis, Mitchell (1993 ch 3) argued that psychoanalysis was going through a paradigm change. He did so in his special reflective, open-minded, theoretically and conceptually brilliant, but nonaggressive style, without falling into the trap of sectarianism that had characterized psychoanalysis for most of its history. Mitchell was soon recognized as the unofficial leader of a new psychoanalytic movement positioned in two new institutions: the relational track at the New York University Postdoctoral Program in Psychotherapy and Psychoanalysis and the journal *Psychoanalytic Dialogues* (see Aron 1996 ch 1).

Jessica Benjamin's (1989) *The Bonds of Love* was to reach way beyond the bounds of the psychoanalytic community. This book is an intricate examination of several core issues in psychoanalysis. How is the human subject constituted in a dialectical process of mutual recognition first of mother and child and then of human subjects in general? How do seemingly "natural" conceptions of gender really reflect ways in which this process of mutual recognition has been distorted in patriarchal societies? How is female masochism really a reflection of social structures of domination? Benjamin has woven a critical reading of Freud's psychosexual theory, Winnicott's concept of the use of the object, feminist theory, and Hegelian philosophy into an intricate and compelling integrative theoretical framework that continues to evolve to this very day.

Lewis Aron's (1996) *A Meeting of Minds: Mutuality in Psychoanalysis* gives an account of how a new movement emerged that blends the passion of a participant in the new movement with a surprisingly early historical sense of how the movement emerged. His book puts the emphasis squarely on what, arguably, is the center of relational thinking: the concept, and as I claim, the ethos of mutuality.

The relational school has made a sustained and impressive effort to rethink the concept of psychoanalytic authority. Its major figures, such as the late Stephen Mitchell, Lewis Aron, Irwin Z. Hoffman, and others, have integrated into a new psychoanalytic paradigm the cultural values of feminism, the postmodern critique of claims to unique authority on truth, and the politics of identity.

Even though theoretical and clinical questions are at the heart of the now vast corpus of relational thought (see Mitchell and Aron 1999), I believe that also at its heart is a new ethos.

Seemingly technical issues like how much and in what form analysts should share their feelings and thoughts with patients, and intricate theoretical analyses of the ways in which human subjects mutually constitute each other both in life and the analytic consulting room, have heralded a new value structure.

The relational ethos integrated many central cultural developments into psychoanalysis. A highly sophisticated version of feminist thought was both incorporated and further developed. A keen awareness of the cultural construction of gender was fused with the psychoanalytic emphasis on the experience of the body. The postmodern deconstruction of conceptions of authority was used to reexamine the nature of psychoanalytic knowledge and authority.

What unites this mode of thinking and experiencing is not necessarily a single theoretical credo. Relational thinkers range from Freudian through strongly Winnicottian to overtly mystical and Buddhist leanings. At the heart of relational thinking lies a deeply democratic impulse. This movement seeks to explore what it means that human beings can live in a way that truly recognizes the other's existence, and the way in which human lives are enmeshed with each other while maintaining distinct individuality.

In this respect, relational thinking tried to address the large-scale issues that faced Western societies toward the end of the 20th and at the beginning of the 21st century. After the horrors of totalitarianism, genocide, and the Cold War, much political thinking was geared to questioning how these aberrations could be avoided. How could groups and individuals respect their differences while maintaining the possibility for dialogue? How could societies share basic ethical values without infringing on identities defined by religion, ethnicity, gender, or sexual orientation?

Relational psychoanalysis brought these issues into focus by reexamining psychoanalytic developmental thought. Using contemporary research on mother-infant attachment, it has tried to show that mutuality existed from the very beginning of life, that infants are not just passive receivers of maternal care, but active participants in a process of mutual regulation. Through detailed analyses of therapeutic interaction, it has shown how the analytic process is, as Aron

(1996) systematically shows, much more mutual than has ever been envisaged.

Relational psychoanalysis did connect to some European philosophical traditions. Martin Buber's conception of the importance of dialogue in human existence and his concept of the I–thou relationship has been evoked explicitly by Aron (1996). It is no coincidence that the journal most identified with relational psychoanalysis is *Psychoanalytic Dialogues,* which often takes the format of psychoanalysts conducting a dialogue on its pages. In this way, the model of solitary thinkers who develop their ideas is replaced by that of a community of practitioners and writers who develop their ideas in constant interaction.

The relational movement attempts to integrate a truly democratic vision of mutuality of recognition into psychoanalysis both theoretically and clinically. Because this vision is, I believe, very much a historically new phenomenon, foreshadowed only by 19th-century liberal thought (Mill 1859) but coming to fruition very lately, I will not try to link it to a Greco-Roman school of thought and life.

Nevertheless, relational psychoanalysis is first and foremost an ethos. It addresses questions of human life that have moved into focus in recent political thought (Giddens 1993). How can humans live together in the dialectics of mutuality and difference? How can we relate to each other as objects of love without negating each other's subjectivities? How can we exercise authority (whether as psychoanalysts, as educators, or as economic and political leaders) while accepting the perspective of the other (analysand, student, employee, or citizen) as legitimate? How can we compete with each other without infringing on each other's rights? In that sense, the relational movement is the integration of modern politics into the psychoanalytic consulting room and psychoanalytic theory.

LOOKING FOR A SENSE OF AUTHORSHIP, OR, WHERE FREUD MEETS SARTRE

There is a philosophical school of recent origin that might prove to be an interesting addition to psychoanalytic discourse. Existentialism had its heyday in the 1940s and 1950s. It was a dominant force in continental European philosophy and, in the case of Sartre, became a focal voice in French culture (Levy 2000). There was also an important existential movement in psychiatry and psychotherapy that originated in the work of Ludwig Binswanger. Its impact was dramatically cut short by the emergence of the Third Reich, and the existentialist and Daseinsanalytic school, based on the thinking of Martin Heidegger, lost much of its impact; it survived primarily in Switzerland, the only German-speaking country not ruled by the Nazis.

A revival of existentialist thought in the United States was sparked primarily by the seminal volume *Existence,* edited by Rollo May and Henri Ellenberger (1958). But it is fair to say that this movement has lost much of its impact in the last 20 years.

In Europe existentialism came under strong attack by the then fashionable structuralist and poststructuralist movements from the 1960s onward. The "in" thing was to deconstruct the subject, and the existentialist emphasis on phenomenological investigation of the structure of human existence began to seem quaintly naïve, nothing but a legacy of the Eurocentric tendency to overlook the many ways in which the subject is really a cultural construct.

Nevertheless, in the historical present a renewed interest in existentialism may turn out to be fruitful for psychoanalysis. Along with philosopher Arthur Danto (1975), I consider Sartre's (1943) *Being and Nothingness* to be one of the towering works of 20th-century philosophy. His phenomenological analyses of the relationship of subjectivity and corporeality; his views on the complexity of intersubjective relationships, as well as his more specific analyses of phenomena like sadism and masochism, remain among the masterpieces of European thought.

In particular, I would like to highlight Sartre's analysis of the temporality of human existence. He emphasized that there is an intrinsic dialectical paradox in human existence: human beings are *situated.* By this, Sartre meant that the base materials of individual human lives are neither chosen nor created by human subjects. We are, as Heidegger (1927) and Sartre (1943) said, *thrown* into existence.

Nevertheless, the human imagination always transcends the immediate situation. We can always imagine things to have been different. The intrinsic tension of human existence is to come to terms with the tension between thrownness and human freedom. Human freedom consists not in the possibility to create ourselves from scratch, but, rather, in the way we interpret our history in a constant process of projecting ourselves into the future.

Much contemporary psychoanalytic thought revolves around intersubjectivity and the crucial impact it has on the formation and structure of the individual psyche. As opposed to that Sartre always emphasized that the existence of the Other is also a curse—a view very much reflected, from a different vantage point, in Lacan's (1977) thinking. Sartre felt that other human beings, although indispensable, always limit individual freedom. Moreover, he tried to show that there is something in the ontological structure of human existence that can never fully accept our dependence on others, even though this dependence can never be abolished.

Sartre and Lacan spent their lives expounding views opposed to harmonistic conceptions of human existence. For both, the ontology of the human subject is fraught with insoluble tensions. In Sartre's philosophy, it is the tension between *pour soi* (the intangibility and reflexivity of human consciousness) and *en soi* (the corporeality of human beings). For Lacan, it is the irreducible tension between our animal provenance and the nexus of cultural laws that makes us human.

I believe that opening a dialogue with Sartre's philosophy might enable us to find deeper and more fruitful ways to analyze the dialectics of human relations. I see the beginnings of such an analysis in Benjamin's (1990) analysis of intersubjectivity as a dialectic between recognition and destruction. Benjamin's thought, fusing that of Hegel and Winnicott, acknowledges that intersubjectivity is far from being a purely harmonious relationship.

Sartre might prove to be a fascinating addition to our understanding of the tensions and paradoxes of human lives. I (Strenger 1998) have tried to give a psychoanalytically informed version of Sartre's phenomenological analysis. I tried to restate Sartre's thesis of the irresolvable dialects of existence by arguing that we all need to come to terms with the fact that we are not self-created. The most basic parameters of our lives—our parents, bodies, gender, native language, culture, and the historical circumstances within which we live—are given to us. The question is whether or not we succeed in using these base materials to create and live lives that we truly experience as our own.

To the extent this creation succeeds, human beings live with what I have called a *sense of authorship*. Those who feel that they simply cannot create out of the given base materials a life they experience as their own live with what I have called a *sense of fatedness*. I have tried to show that this terminology bears some resemblance and connection to thoughts developed by Bollas (1989), and they are also connected to basic thoughts formulated by Benjamin (1990).

I have not tried to resolve the dialectic between authorship and fatedness, because, along with Sartre, I take it to be unresolvable. My own, somewhat unwieldy, term for the human experience of this impossibility is *the ontological protest of subjectivity*. There is a core in human experience that cannot fully accept the fact that we are not self-created. Along with Sartre, I believe that human subjectivity contains a core that can never fully accept the world—a thought reflected in Winnicott's (1965) dictum that even in health there is a core of the self that can never quite accept that we have not created ourselves and the world.

These ideas are highly relevant to the historical present. The contemporary view of life and the self as a design project is, in a way, a radicalization of the search for authorship. As we have seen, the cultural demand to experiment with the self and to make it into a free creation is an attempt to push the quest for authorship one step further. It is the attempt to free the human subject from the shackles and limitations imposed by the base materials of life and to create the self anew. In saying this, I do not indict contemporary urban culture for trying to do the impossible. The conception of the self as a design project is a fascinating radicalization of what Sartre and Winnicott took to be an essential feature of human subjectivity.

MORE SCHOOLS, MORE VOICES: TOWARD A NEW PSYCHOANALYTIC CULTURE

Eigen's psychoanalytic mysticism, Phillips's Epicureanism, the relational thought of Mitchell, Benjamin, Aron, and others, and my own attempt to connect existentialism and psychoanalysis are just some of many attempts to create an aesthetic of existence that helps to make sense of human lives in the historical present.

A variety of authors collected in the volume edited by Spezzano and Gargiulio (1997) are trying to find bridges between psychoanalysis and a variety of spiritual and religious traditions. Eigen is one of the major contributors to these attempts. Two other examples are Nina Coltart (1996) and Mark Epstein (1993), who have made valuable integrations between Buddhist thought and practice and psychoanalysis. Symington (1993) has presented a version of psychoanalysis explicitly informed by Judeo-Christian ethics. All these coexist with more traditional schools, like the contemporary Kleinians (Schafer 1997), Freudians, self psychologists of Kohutian persuasion, and interpersonalists. Some may find this plethora of psychoanalytic voices and approaches disconcerting; psychoanalysis is no longer a cohesive body of theory and practice. My own critical pluralism welcomes this variety. Within the bounds of what is consistent with current scientific knowledge, there are many ways to live a full and valuable life.

My own leanings are far from relativist. I have made sustained attempts to explain the difference between relativism and pluralism (Strenger 1991 ch 6). The former is the misguided idea that there is no difference between truth and falsehood, between rigorous and sloppy thinking, between the ethically acceptable and what is to be condemned. Pluralism holds that there are many perspectives on natural and cultural reality that are valid, interesting, and yet not reducible to each other. In the present context, pluralism primarily means that, as in art, there are various forms of life ("life style" is the term for that which constitutes a compelling vision of what it means to live a full and interesting life). Therapeutic narratives, psychoanalytic or otherwise, are versions of such visions of life. Hence, in an age of pluralism, psychoanalysis *needs* a variety of narratives in order to give patients of different creeds, personality characteristics, and personal predilections the possibility of finding therapists who can communicate with them in their own terms.

Looking at psychoanalysis as continuous with Greco-Roman philosophical schools, and as a set of aesthetics of existence, highlights the ethical content of psychoanalysis. Since Freud, psychoanalysis has never been quite comfortable with the idea that it is primarily a form of ethics. Yet every construal of psychic life and of personal development is implicitly guided by an image of what it means to live a good life. If this is true, we might as well feel more comfortable with trying to paint images that help make life worth living.

I believe that this, seemingly anachronistic, conception might be useful for the historical present. If the self is perceived as a design project, various psychoanalytic narratives might be understood as various aesthetics of existence that provide help in the task of recreating the self; and as in the world of art, different aesthetics can coexist with each other in joyful competition rather than by threatening mutual annihilation.

The Place of Psychoanalysis in the Culture of the Designed Self

Finally, a word on the place and function of psychoanalysis in the culture of the designed self. As we have seen through the stories of Iris, Ben, Yaron, Amos, and Ruth, contemporary social arrangements present gifted people entering adulthood with enormous opportunities. The space of freedom they are offered and the amount of experimentation they are invited to engage in are enormous. The variety of new professions, occupations, gender models, and life styles gives more people than ever the chance to shape a life that really suits their inborn potential.

But we also saw the enormous pressure the culture of the designed self puts on precisely those who feel that they might have the potential to live a life that they truly experience as their creation. If there are so many possibilities, then those who do not make use of this space have no one to blame but themselves. So many ways to succeed big time are relentlessly portrayed in the various media and make it difficult to feel that one's achievement is valuable, when compared with the Bill Gateses, the Donald Trumps, the Madonnas, the Paul Austers, the Cindy Crawfords, and the Tom Cruises of this world.

The obsession with success that permeates the culture of the designed self can easily lead to a sense of loss of self. There are epidemiological studies (Buss 1993) that indicate that the incidence of depression and anxiety disorders has quadrupled since the 1970s. Along with Buss, I think that this is partially due to the inundation with images of success. Along with Fukuyama (1999), I believe that many of the social-support structures that help people feel at home in this world have been eroded since the 1970s. And along with Lasch (1979), I think that the focus on the self and the lack of a sense of continuity with earlier generations and the breakdown of a sense of community rob human beings of many resources to sustain themselves psychologically.

The global network of infinite possibilities, and the possibility of designing the self almost without limits, paradoxically can lead to a loss of any sense of self. Iris, Ben, Yaron, Amos, and Ruth all had great abilities and used them productively. Nevertheless, they felt that they were losing rather than finding themselves.

The ritual of the psychoanalytic dialogue, the patient, open-ended exploration of human subjectivity, is in strange contrast to a world that evolves to the tune of Moore's law that computer processors double their speed every two years, in contrast to communication channels, which transmit unlimited amounts of information almost instantaneously.

Psychoanalysis has always insisted that there is a deep self, that the body carries the feeling memory of all our significant interactions in the past, that our unconscious is formed by the suppressed desires of our progenitors even before we were born, that the human psyche always carries more meanings in it than we can bear and be conscious of, and that the cost of shutting out these meanings is a flattening of subjectivity.

In other words, psychoanalysis seems the antithesis of the culture of the designed self. Instead of offering quick fixes for symptoms that inhibit the fast track to success, it insists on listening to the messages those symptoms carry. Instead of trying to short-circuit the brain's biochemistry and thus shut out deeper layers of the self, it attempts to facilitate processes of transformation that allow for the self's complexity to be lived rather than suppressed.

Yet, as I have argued elsewhere (Strenger 1998), the psychoanalytic conception of the deep self and the late modern view of the self as a free creation can interact in a fruitful dialectical tension. I have tried to show that the process of self-creation is not made impossible by the existence of a deep self. Rather, the dialectics between the deep self and one's attempt to shape this deep self into a creation that one feels truly identified with gives the process of self-creation its existential poignancy.

Psychoanalysis need not lament but can add an important voice to the culture of the designed self. The psychoanalytic insistence that tragedy and suffering are not to be wiped out or covered up, that the deep self needs to be integrated into self-creation rather than replaced by it, can bring great relief. The two-dimensionality of flat icons of success is given human depth by the drama of the search for a sense of authorship in life.

By reconnecting those who turn to analysis to various layers of their selves, we need not insist that their projects of self-creation are nothing but unconscious enactments of early object relations or repressed infantile wishes. Instead, we can help patients discover that they can live with their past and transform its sediments in their psyche into their project of self-creation. Hence the psychoanalytic insistence on the existence of a deep self can add a humanizing voice to the open-ended universe of the culture of the designed self.

Requiem to the Dream of Metaphysical Depth: An Epilogue

In my mid-20s I had the following dream:

> It is late evening, I am walking on a road, and I see a two-story house that dates from the 18th century. One room on the first floor is lighted. I approach the house and walk in. I know that in the lighted room Immanuel Kant is dying. I glance into the room. It is lit by candles, and several people are in there, murmuring. The atmosphere is subdued, sad; people try to be with Kant in his dying hours.
>
> I do not enter the room. I am not sure whether I see Kant himself or my inner image of him. I move on. Somehow, from the house I enter a subterranean tunnel that leads me into a subterranean bookstore. It is long, winding and leads deeper and deeper down.

I do not know what book I am looking for. I am likely to find it in the philosophy or maybe (less likely) in the psychology section. My knowledge of what I am seeking is only intuitive. I look for something with depth, something that will quench a deep-seated desire.

> I do not find the book. When I arrive at the exit of the bookstore, I emerge into a passageway. It could either be in Berne, Switzerland's capital, or in the center of Basel, the town of my birth, not far from my father's office.

For 12 or 13 years, I would in dreams return to this bookstore. I would always feel that I knew this bookstore, that I had been there before. The dreams' theme would always be the same in different variations. I was looking for a book, of which I knew neither the title nor the author. What guided me was an almost physical feeling of searching for a deep, hidden truth.

※ ※ ※ ※ ※

My childhood and adolescence were accompanied by books. Most importantly, as part of an orthodox Jewish education, from age five there was the Bible; from age six, the *Mishna,* the older portion of the Talmud; and from age seven, the *Gemarah,* the sections of the Talmud written between the third and sixth century BCE.

The Talmud is supposed to be based entirely on interpretation of Biblical texts. These texts, in turn, are based on immediate revelations by God. The Pentateuch has a special status, as it supposedly was dictated to Moses directly by God. Later Biblical texts are still based on prophetic vision and therefore reflect God's immediate revelation. Hence, the Talmud is a divinely inspired interpretation of the *Torah,* the Bible, which, in turn, is based on immediate revelation of God through the various prophets.

In the *Yeshiva,* men generally study in pairs. You might see them with piles of tomes and rocking their bodies while reciting and arguing in a singsong manner that mirrors the structure of arguments.

Their thought processes could be likened to a cascade of logical lines of thought. They might be comparing contemporary interpreters A and B, who are interpreting interpreters from the 12th century. C is interpreting Talmudic text. D is interpreting a Biblical text. The assumption is that A, B, C, and D are completely consistent. They try out various interpretive lines that would all allow for consistency across the board. They try out these lines to check whether they are entirely consistent with all other occurrences of sayings of those same figures elsewhere in the text. Different interpretive lines have advantages with respect to some saying but create problems with respect to others.

Sitting late into the night interpreting Talmudic texts that, in turn, interpret the Bible creates a fugal structure of interweaving argumentative lines. At the end of these lines is a timeless, ultimate truth emanating directly from the Creator of the world. You might not be able to intuit this ultimate truth directly; but you know that, through the manifold mediation of sages who came progressively closer to TRUTH, you, indirectly, through a looking glass only, partake of TRUTH.

Hence, whatever questions you may have about how to live, what is valuable, and what is important, immersing yourself in these texts is of indisputable value. By doing so you fulfill your Creator's wish and do something that need not be questioned.

※ ※ ※ ※ ※

In the dream, I emerge in a place that could be close to my father's office, which I loved to visit as a child. It gave me a special sense of connection to my father, to his professional competence and the human qualities he brought to bear in his relationships with his clients. Alternatively, I might end up in Berne. The last time I visited Berne was with my father– around the time I dreamt the dream. I cherish the memory of that trip, which was carefree and enjoyable, and I remember the present he bought me there.

Clearly, the search for *the* book is connected to my father's legacy: Orthodox Judaism combined with respect and admiration for the Canon of Western Culture. The first part of that legacy I rejected; the second will stay with me throughout my life.

※ ※ ※ ※ ※

After that fateful morning after my 18th birthday, when I had the crystal clear, icy thought, "There is no God," and began my journey into a secular mode of life, the metaphysical foundation of the value of reading these texts disappeared.

But the sense of bliss, the intuitive belief that there are books that promise to make you partake of some ultimate truth, was engrained in my soul. For many years I would transfer this bliss, this desire for ultimate truth, to other texts. First and foremost to philosophy; the discipline that has purported for at least two millennia to formulate the ultimate truth about the world; second, to psychoanalysis, which purports to formulate the deepest truth about the human psyche, and therefore about life.

※ ※ ※ ※ ※

There are few texts in the history of Western philosophy that invite the sense of getting in touch with some deep, ultimate truth as deeply as Kant's *Critique of Pure Reason,* first published in 1781. The sense of deep, ultimate truth engendered by this book entails a certain paradox. The most basic thesis of *Critique of Pure Reason* is that human thought cannot possibly apprehend *reality* itself. Any thought about the world is shaped by the basic structures of human thought, and every perception of the world reflects the a priori structure of human sensibility. Hence, inevitably, human beings can apprehend only appearances and never the thing in itself.

Kant buried the dream of Western metaphysics that the human mind, through correct reasoning, can discover the ultimate structure of reality. Kant thus became the culmination of the European Enlightenment, whose essence had been the radical critique of human claims to knowledge.

Kant's battle-cry for the enlightenment had been *sapere aude:* dare to know. Most importantly, dare to know the limits of what can be known and accept the finitude of human knowledge. Do not accept any authority that claims to have knowledge of ultimate reality, either by revelation or by reasoning. It is only through this thorough critique of human claims to knowledge that you can aim to liberate yourself from the self-imposed tutelage of the mind.

I first read Kant's *Critique of Pure Reason* at age 18. As this is one of the most difficult (and badly written) texts in the history of Western philosophy, my understanding of it was quite limited at first. I was to return to this text time and again. From age 24 onward, I was to teach it once a year. When I was 25, Kant was the topic of one of my Ph.D. examinations.

Each year, when I opened the text to prepare my classes, I would feel a sense of awe. Each time, for about half an hour, I would have the terrible feeling that I understood absolutely nothing of what was going on there. And then, each year, would arrive the fabulous moment when it all opened up to me: I would reconnect to Kant's intricate line of interweaving arguments that together constituted one of the most intricate, complex, and compelling systems of thought ever devised by a human being.

Of course, there was nothing approaching ultimate truth in Kant's system. Many of his assumptions have turned out to be wrong; his conceptual framework often reflects his compulsive need for order rather than any intrinsic logical necessity. To teach Kant was to show the internal beauty of his reasoning;

but, of necessity, teaching Kant was also to show where his reasoning went wrong. Criticizing Kant mercilessly was the only way of being faithful to his call "dare to know, and liberate yourself from the self-imposed tutelage of the mind." Yet, each year, I tried to get my students to be enthralled by the beauty of Kant's reasoning.

※ ※ ※ ※ ※

As I write these pages, it is close to midnight in a neighborhood café owned by a friend. The stereo is playing hip-hop music. Around me young men and women banter, flirt, chat. I watch the scene as if from a distance. The experiences that I am writing about seem more tangible for me than the friendly, sensual interchanges of those surrounding me. I vaguely remember that often I take part in these exchanges myself, but right now they seem distant, unreal.

I feel the yearning for the deep enthrallment, the endless promise that the search for truth, the enchantment, of the promise of enlightenment once created.

※ ※ ※ ※ ※

In the dream it is night. The street is dark. The building in which Kant is dying has a classic simplicity of design. The room in which Kant lies is lighted by candles.

About an hour ago, it crossed my mind how the dream's iconography metaphorizes the essence of enlightenment: the striving for simplicity; reason as the searchlight that guides both thought and life. It expresses the ethos of liberty and liberation that is at the center of enlightenment thought and practice.

But why is Kant dying?

And why, from his house, do I embark on the one search that he himself argued to be impossible? I seem to be looking for the book that will show me the ultimate truth. By entering the subterranean library, I seem to be trying to pierce the veil of appearances and look for some ultimate, metaphysical truth.

※ ※ ※ ※ ※

In real life I had a passion for books, reflected in the dream of the subterranean bookstore. I looked for the deep texts, those which would give some ultimate enlightenment. And, as in the dream, none of the books actually offered such enlightenment.

Some books did provide deep insights. Paradoxically, those books were primarily by philosophers who argued that the very idea of ultimate knowledge was misguided. Probably one of the books that influenced me more than any other was Richard Rorty's *Philosophy and the Mirror of Nature,* a brilliant combination of analytic philosophy of the highest rank and intellectual history. It is one of those books that truly changed my outlook on life and knowledge.

Rorty's strongest claim in this book is that the metaphor of the mind as reflecting reality is deeply flawed. The mind is not an independent entity, and language does not reflect the world (it is not a mirror of nature). Language is a symbol system embedded in human activity, and its function is to make such activity as useful as possible. Meaning is generated by the ways in which we move and act in the world, not by mental acts of representation. Thinkers like Rorty are deep, but not in the sense that they reach behind appearances to touch hidden reality. Rorty puts what we know in a new context, and as a result we end up seeing everything differently.

Isaiah Berlin's chapter, "Two Concepts of Liberty," in his 1958 collection, *Four Essays on Liberty,* had a similarly profound impact. Berlin's claim was that the idea that all human values cohere into one system, that there is an optimal way of managing human affairs, is not only wrong but a pernicious illusion. The belief in a final solution (Berlin wrote the piece in the years after World War II) is responsible for more suffering than any other human desire. Nothing makes human beings more cruel than the belief that they know where paradise is.

My own writing went in similar directions. My first book argued that psychoanalysis could not produce the type of knowledge it claimed to have. I warned against the tendency of psychoanalysis to ritually reread classical texts as if they contained some timeless truth.

Yet, for years to come, I preferred reading the great classics to reading contemporary authors. Freud himself, enthralling and compelling, provided the ultimate seduction. Authors like Winnicott and Bion seemed to continue the psychoanalytic project of uncovering the deepest levels of the psyche.

I still enjoy reading the classics, particularly Freud, once in a while. But I have lost the belief that classics (*pace* T. S. Eliot) contain a timeless truth. If anything, as Harold Bloom (1994) has argued, they are compelling literary documents that provide rich and rewarding perspectives on life and meaning.

Nevertheless, for years to come, I continued to dream of visits in the subterranean bookstore, and I continued to seek the book that would give me some ultimate truth. My unconscious refused to go along with what I consciously believed, argued for, and defended.

The subterranean bookstore can be seen as a metaphor for the metaphysical depth that has permeated Western thinking. For millennia, metaphysics was enthralled with the distinction between appearance and reality. Reality was hiding behind appearances, and the mind had to penetrate appearances in order to arrive at ultimate truth.

My plight, of course, was not unique. Philosophers like Derrida, while arguing that the search for ultimate reality was a sham, an illusion based on a wrong picture of language, yearned for the truth they denied. Derrida wrote book after book in which he played with the texts that purport to do exactly what he thinks cannot be done. By playing with them, taking them apart, and putting them together again, Derrida performs a protracted ritual of mourning an illusion he had helped to dismantle.

The global culture that forms the background to the individual case studies in this book has done away with depth. Surface is everything, and there is no room for deep truths. Intellectually I agree; the metaphor of depth is misleading. The result of the dismantling of the idea of depth has created flatness. We may have rid ourselves of an illusion. But we may also have rid ourselves of the hope Nietzsche called metaphysical consolation. Contemporary Western culture has gotten rid of a large number of taboos. We saw how the young people I worked with had to find their way in a space more open than any social space that has ever existed. And we saw the difficulty of living with so much freedom.

As a youth I yearned for such openness. I am not sure that I now truly enjoy it. I miss the metaphysical drama that I don't believe in.

To avoid misunderstandings: I do not judge Generation X. I cherish and respect the individual patients I write about. I do not feel that Generation X is a less valuable generation than any other. In any case, they have grown into the cultural reality that they have to deal with. It was the previous generation that deconstructed the metaphysical images, metaphors, and modes of thought and left us with postmodern flatness.

In discussing the postmetaphysical reality we live in, I mourn something that I do not believe in. I recoil from neoconservative reactions that try to return to something that, I believe, is irretrievably dead. I am deeply afraid of the fundamentalist attempts to restore certainties that are, and should be, left behind.

I dreamt variations on the themes of the subterranean library until my late 30s. After that, the dream ceased. On a conscious level, I am no longer enthralled by texts that purport to seek, find, or formulate some deep truths. I finally seem to have gotten rid of the very notion of metaphysical depth, without having given up on the idea of the deep self that is essential to psychoanalysis. Of course there is some relief in this change: I am freer to be interested in the world of appearances.

Nevertheless this epilogue, and, in a sense, this book, is a Requiem to the dream of metaphysical depth.

References

Akhtar, S. (1999), *Immigration and Identity: Turmoil, Treatment and Transformation*. Northvale, NJ: Aronson.

Aron, L. (1996), *A Meeting of Minds: Mutuality in Psychoanalysis*. Hillsdale, NJ: The Analytic Press.

Appignanensi, L. & Forrester, J. (1992), *Freud's Women*. London: Weidenfeld & Nicholson.

Avineri, S. (1980), *Varieties of Zionist Thought*. Tel Aviv: Am Oved.

Beaudoin, T. (1998), *Virtual Faith: The Irreverent Spiritual Quest of Generation X*. New York: Jossey-Bass.

Bell, D. (1966), *The End of Ideology*. New York: Basic Books.

Benjamin, J. (1989), *The Bonds of Love: Feminism, Psychoanalysis and the Problem of Domination*. New York: Pantheon.

——— (1990), Recognition and destruction: An outline of intersubjectivity. *Psychoanalytic Psychology*, 7(suppl):33–47.

——— (1995), *Like Subjects, Love Objects*. New Haven, CT: Yale University Press.

Ben-Ami, S. (1998), *A Place for All*. Hakibbutz: Hameuchad.

Berlin, I. (1951), The hedgehog and the fox. In: *Russian Thinkers*. Harmondsworth, UK: Penguin, 1978, pp. 22-81.

——— (1958), Two concepts of liberty. In: *Four Essays on Liberty*. Oxford: Oxford University Press, pp. 118–172.

Bloom, A. (1987), *The Closing of the American Mind*. New York: Simon & Schuster.

Bloom, H. (1973), *The Anxiety of Influence*. Oxford: Oxford University Press.

——— (1994), *The Western Canon*. New York: Free Press.

Bollas, C. (1989), *Forces of Destiny: Psychoanalysis and Human Idiom*. New York: Aronson.

——— (1992), *On Being a Character*. New York: Hill & Wang.

——— (1997), Interview with Andrew Molino. In: *Freely Associated: Encounters in Psychoanalysis with Christopher Bollas, Joyce McDougall, Michael Eigen, Adam Phillips, Nina Coltart*, ed. A. Molino. London: Free Association Books.

——— (2000), *Hysteria*. London: Routledge.

Brooks, D. (2000), *Bobos (Bourgeois Bohemians) in Paradise: The New Upper Class and How They Got There*. New York: Simon & Schuster.

Brown, N. (1959), *Life against Death*. Middletown, CT: Wesleyan University Press.

Bushnell, C. (1996), *Sex in the City.* New York: Warner Books.

Buss, D. M (1993), *The Evolution of Desire: Strategies of Human Mating.* New York: Basic Books.

Buswell, R. (1992), *The Zen Monastic Experience.* Princeton, NJ: Princeton University Press.

Chasseguet-Smirgel, J. (1984), *Creativity and Perversion.* London: Free Association Books.

Chodorow, N. (1979), *The Reproduction of Mothering.* Berkeley: University of California Press.

——— (1994), *Femininities, Masculinities, Sexualities.* London: Free Association Books.

Coltart, N. (1996), *The Baby and the Bathwater.* London: Karnac.

Danto, A. (1975), *Sartre.* London: Fontana Masters Series.

Edlis, G. (2003), The subjective experience of life-cycle in homosexuals. Unpublished M.A. thesis, Tel Aviv University.

Ehrlich, J. R. & Rehfeld, B. J. (1989), *The New Crowd: The Changing of the Jewish Guard on Wall Street.* Boston, MA: Little, Brown.

Eigen, M. (1993), *The Electrified Tightrope,* ed. A, Phillips. Northvale, NJ: Aronson.

——— (1996), *Psychic Deadness.* Northvale, NJ: Aronson.

——— (1997), Interview with Andrew Molino. In: *Freely Associated: Encounters in Psychoanalysis with Christopher Bollas, Joyce McDougall, Michael Eigen, Adam Phillips, Nina Coltart,* ed. A. Molino. London: Free Association Books.

——— (1998), *The Psychoanalytic Mystic.* London: Free Association Books.

——— (2002), *Ecstasy.* Middletown, CT: Wesleyan University Press.

Eisenstadt, S. N. (1985), *The Transformation of Israeli Society.* London: Weidenfels & Nicholson.

Eliade, M. (1947), *The Sacred and the Profane.* Chicago: University of Chicago Press.

Eliot, T. S. (1975), *Selected Prose of T. S. Eliot,* ed. F. Kermode. London: Faber.

Ellenberger, H. (1970), *The Discovery of the Unconscious.* New York: Basic Books.

Ellis, B. E. (1991), *American Psycho.* New York: Simon & Schuster.

Epstein, M. (1993), *Thoughts Without a Thinker.* New York: Basic Books.

Erikson, E. H. (1950), *Childhood and Society.* New York: Norton.

——— (1968), *Identity, Youth and Crisis.* New York: Norton.

Ferenczi, S. (1987), *The Clinical Diary of Sándor Ferenczi,* ed. J. Dupont. Cambridge, MA: Harvard University Press.

Foucault, M. (1961), *Histoire de la folie* [*Madness and Civilization,* trans. R. Howard]. New York: Random House, 1965.

——— (1964), *The Birth of the Clinic: An Archeology of Medical Perception,* trans. A. Sheridan, New York: Random House, 1973.

——— (1966), *The Order of Things: An Archeology of the Human Sciences,* trans. A. Sheridan. New York: Random House, 1970.

——— (1971), Nietzsche, genealogy, history. In: *The Foucault Reader,* ed. P. Ravinov. New York: Random House, 1984.

——— (1975), *Discipline and Punish: The Birth of the Prison,* trans. A. Sheridan. New York: Random House, 1977.

——— (1976), *The History of Sexuality, Vol. I: An Introduction,* trans. R. Hurley. New York: Random House, 1978.

——— (1983), *The Care of the Self,* trans. R. Hurley. New York: Random House, 1988.

——— (1984), The ethics of the concern of the self as a practice of freedom, In: *The Essential Foucault, Vol. 1: Ethics,* ed. P. Rabinov. New York: Pantheon, 1997, pp. 281-301.

Freud, S. (1915), Observations on transference love. *Standard Edition,* 12:157-171. London: Hogarth Press, 1958.

——— (1930), Civilization and its discontents. *Standard Edition,* 21:59-148. London: Hogarth Press, 1961.

Friedman, T. (1999), *The Lexus and the Olive Tree.* New York: Farrar, Straus & Giroux.

Frum, D. (1999), *How We Got Here: The 70's: The Decade that Brought You Modern Life—For Better or Worse.* New York: Basic Books.

Fukuyama, F. (1992), *The End of History and the Last Man.* New York: Free Press.

——— (1999), *The Great Disruption: Human Nature and the Reconstitution of Social Order.* New York: Simon & Schuster.

Gaskin, J. (1995), *The Epicurean Philosophers.* New York: Everyman Library.

Gay, P. (1988), *Freud: A Life for Our Times.* New York: Norton.

Gedo, J. (1979), *Beyond Interpretation: Toward a Revised Theory for Psychoanalysis.* Hillsdale, NJ: The Analytic Press, 1993.

Gellner, E. (1985), *The Psychoanalytic Movement: The Cunning of Unreason (Rethinking Theory).* London: Fonatana.

Gergen, K. (1991), *The Saturated Self: Dilemmas of Identity in Contemporary Life.* New York: Basic Books.

Giddens, A. (1993), *Beyond Left and Right: The Future of Radical Politics.* New York: Polity.

Gilman, S. (1986), *Jewish Self-Hatred.* Baltimore., MD: Johns Hopkins University Press.

——— (1993), *The Case of Sigmund Freud: Medicine and Identity at the Fin de Siècle.* Baltimore, MD: Johns Hopkins University Press.

Gorkin, M. (1987), *The Uses of Countertransference.* New York: Aronson.

Gross, P. (1999), *Ich Jagd.* Frankfurt: Suhrkamp.

Grosskurth, P. (1986), *Melanie Klein.* London, Maresfield.

Hadot, P. (1995), *Philosophy as a Way of Life: Spiritual Exercises from Socrates to Foucault,* ed. A. Davidson (trans. M. Chase). Oxford: Blackwell.

Heidegger, M. (1927), *Sein und Zeit.* Tübingen: Niemeyer.

Hillman, J. (1975), *Re-Visioning Psychology.* New York: HarperCollins.

——— (1996), *The Soul's Code: In Search of Character and Calling.* New York: Random House.

Himmelfarb, G. (1999), *One Nation, Two Cultures.* New York: Knopf.

Hobsbawm, E. (1994), *The Age of Extremes: A History of the World 1914-1991.* New York: Pantheon.

Hoffman, I. Z. (1983), The patient as interpreter of the analyst's experience. In: *Relational Psychoanalysis: The Emergence of a Tradition,* ed. S. A. Mitchell & L. Aron. Hillsdale, NJ: The Analytic Press, 1999, pp. 39-75.

——— (1999), *Ritual and Spontaneity in Psychoanalysis.* Hillsdale, NJ: The Analytic Press.

Holtz, J. T. (1995), *Welcome to the Jungle: The Why Behind "Generation X."* New York: St. Martin's Press.

Huntington, S. (1999), *The Clash of Civilization and the Remaking of a New World Order.* New York: Pantheon.

Juno, A. & Vale, V. (1995), *Urban Aboriginals.* New York: Research Press.

Kant, I. (1783), Was ist Aufklaerung? In: *Immanuel Kant, Schriften zur Anthropologie, Bd I.* Frankfurt: Suhrkamp, 1964.

Kermode, F. (1994), Advance praise of A. Phillips's *On Flirtation.* Cambridge, MA: Harvard University Press.

Kimball, R. (2000), *The Long March: How the Cultural Revolution of the 1960s Changed America.* San Francisco: Encounter Books.

Klein, M. (1952), The origins of transference. In: *Envy and Gratitude and Other Works, 1946–1963.* New York: Basic Books.

Kohut, H. (1971), *The Analysis of the Self.* Madison, CT: International Universities Press.

——— (1977), *The Restoration of the Self.* Madison, CT: International Universities Press.

Kristeller, P. O. (1979), *Renaissance Thought and Its Sources.* New York: Columbia University Press.

Kristeva, J. (1993), *The New Maladies of the Soul,* trans. R. Guberman. New York: Columbia University Press.

Lacan, J. (1977), *Ecrits: A Selection,* trans. & selected A. Sheridan. New York: Norton.

Laertius, D. (1925), *Lives of Eminent Philosophers,* trans. R. D. Hicks. Cambridge, MA: Harvard University Press.

Lasch, C. (1979), *The Culture of Narcissism.* New York: Norton.

Levy, J. B. (2000), *Le Siècle de Sartre.* Paris: Grasset.

Loewald, H. (1960), On the therapeutic action of psychoanalysis. In: *Papers on Psychoanalysis.* New Haven, CT: Yale University Press, 1980, pp. 221–256.

Lyotard, F. (1979), *The Postmodern Condition.* Oxford: Blackwell.

Marcuse, H. (1955), *Eros and Civilization.* Boston, MA: Little, Brown.

May, R. & Ellenberger, H. (1958), *Introduction to Existence,* ed. R. May & H. Ellenberger. New York: Basic Books.

Mill, J. S. (1859), *On Liberty.* Harmondsworth: Penguin, 1964.

Mitchell, S. (1993), *Hope and Dread in Psychoanalysis.* New York: Basic Books.

——— (1997), *Autonomy and Influence in Psychoanalysis.* New York: Basic Books.

——— & Aron, L., eds. (1999), *Relational Psychoanalysis: The Emergence of a Tradition.* Hillsdale, NJ: The Analytic Press.

Mitscherlich, A. (1967), *Auf dem Weg zur Vaterlosen Gesellschaft.* Munich: Piper.

Molino, A., ed. (1997), *Freely Associated: Encounters in Psychoanalysis with Christopher Bollas, Joyce McDougall, Michael Eigen, Adam Phillips, Nina Coltart.* London: Free Association Books.

Montaigne, M. (1958), *Essays,* trans. J. M. Cohen. Harmondsworth: Penguin Classical Library.

Morris, B. (2001), *Righteous Victims.* New York: Vintage.

Nehamas, A. (1985), *Nietzsche: Life as Literature.* Cambridge, MA: Harvard University Press.

Nietzsche, F. (1884), *The Gay Science,* trans. W. Kaufmann. New York: Vintage Press.

Noll, R. (1994), *The Jung Cult.* Princeton, NJ: Princeton University Press.

Nussbaum, M. (1995), *The Therapy of Desire.* Princeton, NJ: Princeton University Press.

——— (1997), *Cultivating Humanity.* Cambridge, MA: Harvard University Press.

Ogden, T. (1995), *The Primitive Edge of Experience.* Northvale, NJ: Aronson.

Omer, H. (1999), *Non-violent Resistance: A New Approach to Violent and Self-Destructive Children.* Cambridge: Cambridge University Press.

Orbach, A. O. & Greenberg, N. S., eds. (2000), *The Working Alliance: Theory, Research and Practice.* New York: Wiley.

——— & Simons, B. D. (1991), Relation between working alliance and outcome in psychotherapy. Meta-analysis: *J. Counsel.,* 38:139–149.

Orlensky, B. E., Grawe, K. & Park, B. K. (1994), Process and outcome in psychotherapy: Noch einmal. In: *Handbook of Psychotherapy and Behavior Change,* ed. S. A. Bergin & S. Garfield. New York: Wiley, pp. 270–370.

Paglia, C. (1990), *Sexual Personae.* New Haven, CT: Yale University Press.

Phillips, A. (1993), *On Kissing, Tickling and Being Bored.* London: Faber.

——— (1994), *On Flirtation: Psychoanalytic Essays on the Uncommitted Life.* Cambridge, MA: Harvard University Press.

——— (1995), *Terrors and Experts.* London: Faber.

——— (1999), *Darwin's Worms.* New York: Basic Books.

Rorty, R. (1979), *Philosophy and the Mirror of Nature.* Princeton, NJ: Princeton University Press.

Roszak, T. (1969), *The Making of a Counterculture.* Berkeley: University of California Press.

Roth, A. & Fonagy, P. (1996), *What Works for Whom? A Critical Review of Psychotherapy Research.* New York: Guilford.

Roudinesco, E. (1996), *Jacques Lacan,* trans. B. Bray. New York: Columbia University Press.

Sachar, H. M. (1986), *The Course of Modern Jewish History,* rev. New York: Vintage.

Said, E. (1979), *The Question of Palestine.* New York: Time Books.

Sartre, J-P. (1943), *L'être et le néant [Being and Nothingness],* trans. H. Barnes. New York: Random House, 1956.

Schafer, R (1983), *The Analytic Attitude.* New York: Basic Books.

——— ed. (1997), *The Contemporary Kleinians of London.* Madison, CT: International Universities Press.

Seabrook, J. (2000), *Nobrow: The Culture of Marketing and the Marketing of Culture.* New York: Knopf.

Seigel, J. (1986), *Bohemian Paris: Culture, Politics and the Boundaries of Bourgeois Life, 1830–1930.* Baltimore, MD: Johns Hopkins University Press.

Shapira, A. (1997), *New Jews, Old Jews.* Tel Aviv: Am Oved.

Shlaim, A. (1998), *The Iron Wall: Israel and the Arab World.* New York: Norton

Sloterdijk, P. (1996), *Selbstversuch: Gespräche mit Carlos Oliveira*. Frankfurt: Suhrkamp.

Spezzano, C. & Gargiulo, G. J., eds. (1987), *Soul on the Couch: Spirituality, Religion, and Morality in Contemporary Psychoanalysis*. Hillsdale, NJ: The Analytic Press.

Stoller, R. (1991), *Pain and Passion: A Psychoanalyst Explores the World of S&M*. New York: Plenum.

Stolorow, R., Brandchaft, B. & Atwood, G. (1987), *Psychoanalytic Treatment: An Intersubjective Approach*. Hillsdale, NJ: The Analytic Press.

Strenger, C. (1989), The classic and the romantic vision in psychoanalysis. *Internat. J. Psycho-Anal.*, 70:593–610.

——— (1991), *Between Hermeneutics and Science: An Essay on the Epistemology of Psychoanalysis*. Madison, CT: International Universities Press.

——— (1997), Hedgehogs, foxes and critical pluralism: On the clinician's yearning for unified conceptions. *Psychoanal. Contemp. Thought*, 20:111-145.

——— (1998), *Individuality, the Impossible Project: Psychoanalysis and Self Creation*. New York: Other Press, 2002.

——— (2002a), *The Quest for Voice in Contemporary Psychoanalysis*. Madison, CT: International Universities Press.

——— (2002b), From Yeshiva to critical pluralism: Reflections on the impossible project of individuality. *Psychoanal. Inq.*, 22:534–558

Symington, N. (1993), *Narcissism: A New Theory*. London: Karnac Books.

Taylor, C. (1989), *Sources of the Self*. Cambridge, MA: Harvard University Press.

Thau, R. & Heflin, J., eds. (1997), *Generations Apart: Xers vs Boomers, vs the Elderly*. New York: Prometheus Books.

Time Out (2001), The guide to single life, Mar. 7.

Weininger, O. (1903), *Sex and Character*. New York: Howard Fertig.

Weiss, J. & Sampson, H. (1986), *The Psychoanalytic Process: Theory, Clinical Observation, and Empirical Research*. New York: Guilford Press.

Wiesel, E. (1984), *Souls on Fire*. Harmondsworth: Penguin Books.

Winnicott, D. W. (1960), Ego distortions in terms of true and false self. In: *The Maturational Processes and the Facilitating Environment*. Madison, CT: International Universities Press, 1965, pp. 140–152.

——— (1965), *The Maturational Processes and the Facilitating Environment*. Madison, CT: International Universities Press.

——— (1969), The use of an object and relating through identification. In: *Playing and Reality*. New York: Basic Books, 1971, pp. 86–94.

——— (1971), *Playing and Reality*. New York: Basic Books.

Wittgenstein, L. (1953), *Philosophical Investigations*, trans. E. Anscombe. Oxford: Blackwell.

Wolfe, T. (1986), *The Bonfire of the Vanities*. New York: Vintage.

Yalom, I. (1980), *Existential Psychotherapy*. New York: Basic Books.

Zakaria, F. (2003), *The Future of Freedom: Illiberal Democracy Abroad and at Home*. New York: Norton.

Index

R

S